THE
CORPORATE AIRCRAFT
OWNER'S HANDBOOK

D1711927

Other TAB books by the author:

Acknowledgements

I wish to thank the following companies for supplying illustrations used in this book: Cessna, Beech, Gates Learjet, Piper, Canadair, Mooney, Rockwell International, Swearingen, Mitsubishi, Bell Helicopter, Boeing Vertol, Sikorsky, Hughes Helicopters and Israel Aircraft Industries.

THE
CORPORATE AIRCRAFT
OWNER'S HANDBOOK

BY PAUL GARRISON

MODERN AVIATION SERIES

TAB BOOKS Inc.

BLUE RIDGE SUMMIT, PA. 17214

FIRST EDITION

FIRST PRINTING

Copyright © 1981 by TAB BOOKS Inc.

Printed in the United States of America

Library of Congress Cataloging in Publication Data

Garrison, Paul.
    The corporate aircraft owner's handbook.

    Includes index.
    1. Airplanes, Company—Handbooks, manuals, etc.
I. Title.
TL722.G37   387.7′   80-21128
ISBN 0-8306-9665-2
ISBN 0-8306-2296-9 (pbk.)

Cover photo courtesy of Piper Aircraft Corp.

Contents

Introduction

Eye contact. That's what it's all about. Despite all the incredibily sophisticated means of instant communication which we have at our disposal, no important sale is ever made or no major contrast or agreement negotiated without having two or more principal executives face one another in direct contact. In years past it was generally accepted tradition that businesses and companies of any size would locate in major cities, erecting their factories as near to that city as was feasible. In those days cities provided conveniences which were not available elsewhere. They were the only places where goods and services were easily available, and face-to-face communication could be achieved by walking or driving from one corporate headquarters building to another. But things have changed. The so-called middle classes have found city living increasingly distasteful and the environment an unhealthly one in which to raise children. Thus started the move to the suburbs and with it the hours of daily commuting from the "bedroom community" to the office.

Corporate Aviation

Today the importance of the major city as a focal point of commerce and industry is rapidly diminishing. More and more large national and international corporations have moved their headquarters as well as their manufacturing facilities to smaller communities less plagued by traffic jams, power outages, pollution and crime. A New York or Chicago address is no longer a status symbol, and skilled employees, engineers, designers, scientists and salesmen are ever more willing to relocate in these more livable communities.

But the need for eye contact, for face-to-face communication, has not diminished. It simply has evolved into a system of efficient

8

on-demand transportation, one which can rarely be satisfied by the automobile or the commercial airlines. Thus, there has been phenomenal growth in recent years of what is generally referred to as corporate and business aviation. Like the electric typewriter, the Xerox machine, the WATS (wide area telephone service) line and the computer, the airplane has simply evolved into a business machine, a necessary tool, now stripped of its former aura of being a status symbol or a luxury toy of the super rich.

The airplane means quick and convenient access to any place anywhere in the country or, for that matter, in the world. The airlines, while still serving several hundred communities in the United States, provide this service with any convenient frequency only between about a half dozen major hubs in the country. The automobile, hobbled by the 55-mph (miles per hour) speed limit, is no longer a viable means of transportation when distances of any consequence are involved. The railroads have long been considered more or less obsolete in terms of passenger transport, and no self-respecting businessman or executive would be caught dead going by Greyhound or Trailways.

The company-owned airplane, on the other hand, is ready and available whenever and wherever it is needed. It is not hampered by speed limits and, with over 10,000 airports and landing places at its disposal, can take its pilot and passengers reasonably close to any likely destination.

Justifying Aircraft Ownership

In order to justify aircraft ownership, a company need not be a multi-national corporation with gross sales running into the billions of dollars. Any reasonably healthy company with a growth potential, and the desire to realize that potential, will sooner or later find that an airplane, possibly a very modest single-engine one to start, will open heretofore undreamed of vistas of opportunity.

As an example, some years ago a group of fellows who owned a little hardware store somewhere in North Carolina, but who had some big ideas about the potential of their strictly local business, happened to run into a pilot who owned a Cessna 172. They asked him what he would charge to fly them around some promising neighboring towns so that they could look for some promising locations for other hardware stores. He quoted a figure which seemed reasonable and so they took off. As a result of this first flight they did open several other stores in the area. The men soon hired that same pilot and his airplane to provide them with quick and convenient transportation between the various locations.

That was some 15 years ago. Today this same company operates close to 100 stores in 14 eastern states, reporting an annual gross revenue in the neighborhoood of $200,000,000. Granted, the transformation from a single hardware store into this far-flung operation involved more than just the intelligent use of aircraft. There was forward looking management which used liberal employee benefit and profit sharing plans to attract and retain top quality employees. A computer network was installed to provide quick and reliable record keeping and communication. The venerable 172 was replaced by a fleet of larger and faster aircraft to move skilled people, regardless of their position on the management or salary scale, to locations where they are needed. And then there is a fleet of company-owned trucks to move freight.

But one thing is certain. Without the use of the airplane, none of this could ever have been realized. Today the company's aviation department, under the guidance of that same pilot who made that first flight, has developed into a highly sophisticated operation. Owning two turboprops and two piston twins, it makes the aircraft available to anyone who has a legitimate need to travel. For five days, sometimes six, each week, each airplane is likely to spend more time in the air than on the ground. The company computer keeps track of all aircraft movements, helps to schedule each airplane to minimize deadhead time, and keeps track of operating costs in terms of overall expense as well as in terms of cost per passenger mile. Because of the high ultilization of the airplanes, this cost is often less than it would be using any other means of transportation.

Quite often, when companies are first faced with the rather considerable expense involved in aircraft acquisition and operation, they find it difficult to justify the cost in terms which make sense to the comptroller or accountant. In this book we will examine these costs in detail and try to relate them to the very real advantages obtained in terms of time and productivity. We will outline ways and means by which a businessman can get into business aviation without spending an arm and a leg. We will try and analyze what kind of aircraft is the right one for which type of transportation need, and we will compare the cost of operating aircraft with that of using alternate means of locomotion. Also, we will deal with the problems of intelligent scheduling and of aviation department management.

Paul Garrison

Chapter 1

Business Aircraft and Travel Needs

When we decide as individuals to purchase an airplane, we rarely worry about justifying its cost of acquisition and subsequent operation in terms of dollars saved. We have learned to accept the fact that airplanes are expensive and, figuring purely the dollars and cents involved, it is often cheaper to get just about anywhere using other means of transportation, such as the airlines or the automobile. But once this aircraft is considered a business machine, its justification, in the light of the overall profit and loss picture of our business or corporation, will become necessary to justify it to tax accountants as well as stockholders (Figs. 1-1 and 1-2).

Advantages of Corporate Aircraft Ownership

What are the basic advantages of business or corporate aircraft ownership? Above all, the intelligent utilization of business aircraft, be it a Skyhawk or a Learjet, produces vastly increased mobility for persons who need to travel in order to maintain or improve the competitive position of the company (Fig. 1-3). Conversely it reduces the amount of time wasted due to poor schedules, waiting at airports, and unnecessary evenings and nights spent away from home. To many executives it is a major consideration in deciding whether to join a company or to accept offers from a competing company. In other words, business aircraft have proven useful in attracting high-caliber management talent.

But, in order to justify the ownership of one or several business aircraft, it is important to analyze the company's travel needs. Based on those data, it is then possible to decide on the type of aircraft which the company should own and the kind and flight schedule which should be maintained.

Fig. 1-1. Business aviation has experienced a phenomenal growth in recent years.

Analyzing Travel Necessities

A relatively simple way to accomplish this is to make up a chart that lists all trips, paid for by the company, which were made during a recent 12-month period. Include those trips involving company personnel, customers, consultants or anyone else. If someone in the comapny owns his own airplane, all trips using it made for the benefit of, and therefore paid by, the company should be included.

Table 1-1 shows such a chart. On the top are the various points of departure and down the left are the different destinations. Each box has three portions. The bottom portion of each box shows the mileage between each pair of locations. The top portion is used to insert the number of trips made between those two points over the period of 12 months, each single person making the trip regardless of whether it was made alone or whether two persons traveled together, to be figured as one trip. By multiplying the two figures

Fig. 1-2. The company-owned airplane is ready and available when it is needed.

Fig. 1-3. A business aircraft produces increased mobility for persons with a need to travel on business.

we arrive at the passenger miles between each pair of locations which is then entered in the center portion of the box. Then, by adding those totals, we arrive at the aggregate amount of passenger miles paid for by the company in that year.

Determining Average Trip Lengths

The next step involves determining average trip lengths. If most trips involve distances of 500 miles or less, aircraft ranging from high performance singles to cabin-class twins can effectively handle these flights in times comparing favorably with the airlines, assuming that airline service is available between the points in question (Figs. 1-4 and 1-5). If, on the other hand, a high percentage of the flights involves distances in excess of 500 miles, the company might need to consider something a bit faster, such as a turboprop or even a pure jet (Figs. 1-6 and 1-7).

In preparing the sample chart in Table 1-1 we have placed the various points of origin and destination in a consecutive order

Fig. 1-4. Even high performance single-engine aircraft can effectively compete with airline travel on missions of up to 500 miles.

Table 1-1. A Typical Travel-Analysis Chart.

from → to: ↓	ABQ	GUP	PHX	DEN	ORD	ATL	JFK
ABQ	███	23 2392 104	61 16470 270	37 11285 305	11 10802 982	5 5560 1112	3 4653 1551
GUP	25 2600 104	███	0 0 195	3 897 299	0 0 1986	0 0 1250	0 0 1655
PHX	59 15930 270	0 0 195	███	2 1032 516	0 0 1232	1 1372 1372	1 1801 1801
DEN	35 10675 305	3 897 299	2 1032 516	███	2 1620 810	2 2094 1047	1 1349 1349
ORD	11 10802 982	0 0 1986	0 0 1232	2 1620 810	███	0 0 539	1 655 655
ATL	5 5560 1112	0 0 1250	1 1372 1372	2 2094 1047	0 0 539	███	0 0 661
JFK	5 7755 1551	0 0 1655	0 0 1801	0 0 1349	0 0 655	1 661 661	███

Total passenger miles (nm): 122,685   Time of aircraft use (hours) based on 175-knot cruise: 701:03

Fig. 1-5. Cessna's Golden Eagle, a top-of-the-line cabin-class pressurized piston twin.

based on distance rather than by alphabet. This makes it easy to draw a demarcation line around those flights which involve trip lengths of under 500 miles. By dividing the total passenger miles by the cruise speed of the aircraft, we can arrive at the number of hours which the aircraft will be flown. If this total is 300 hours or more, it is a generally accepted rule of thumb that aircraft operation is worthwhile. By contrast, if those total hours come to less than 300, the cost of aircraft ownership and operation may be excessive because of insufficient utilization.

Table 1-1 fails to account for a number of variables. It does not take into account the need of different persons to travel to different locations on the same day. It also fails to include the occasional need to deadhead the airplane or the frequent opportunities for

Fig. 1-6. A turboprop aircraft, such as the Swearingen Merlin, can be economically utilized over long as well as relatively short distances.

15

Fig. 1-7. Pure jets, such as this Learjet, operate most efficiently over longer distances. Their ranges vary from around 1,500 miles to over 3,500 miles.

several persons to combine travel schedules. Still, it is sufficiently accurate to determine if justification for aircraft ownership can be made and, if so, what kind of aircraft should be considered. In the case of the travel schedules represented by Table 1-1, it would seem that the company could actually justify buying and using two airplanes such as a *Cessna 310* or a *Beech Baron* and a *Cheyenne*, or maybe a *Learjet* or *Citation* (Figs. 1-8 through 1-11).

The Problem of Scheduling

It is, of course, a fact that most aircraft purchase decisions by companies other than large corporations are made by the chief executive. He is a pilot and wants to do his business travel in his own airplane. In such cases the aircraft frequently ends up as the president's personal vehicle with little attempt being made to extend its utilization to other company personnel. To remedy this situation the president/pilot should, as much as possible, firm his travel plans for weeks ahead of time and then circulate this information within the compnay. Thus, other persons with a need to travel can adjust their travel schedules accordingly and arrange to go along on the planned trips.

Fig. 1-8. A popular piston twin, the Beech Baron 58.

Fig. 1-9. A medium-priced piston twin, the Cessna 310.

Scheduling is one of the most difficult problems facing any company operating business aircraft. Its requirements vary greatly. If the aircraft is flown by one or several people in the company, the considerations are quite different than they would be at a company which employs one or several professional pilots. And, again, there are vast differences between a single airplane operation and the running of an aviation department responsible for two or more aircraft and the appropriate number of pilots and copilots. However the scheduling is handled, the most effective means of making company aircraft earn their keep is to encourage their use by the largest number of persons within the company with a need to

Fig. 1-10. The Cheyenne III is the top-of-the-line turboprop manufactured by Piper Aircraft Corporation.

Fig. 1-11. The Citation I is the only pure jet aircraft certificated for single-pilot operation.

travel. In analyzing a considerable number of business and corporate aircraft operations, one finds that the healthiest, financially speaking, are those where the aircraft are available to the largest number of persons. Those who use the aircraft purely as an executive chariot may actually find that they are forced to sell it when economic fluctuations call for belt tightening.

Budgeting

Since the various departments within a company usually operate on a budget and are held responsible for keeping within that budget, it tends to be self-defeating to charge each department with a portion of the cost of aircraft operation, commensurate with the amount of use made of the aircraft by department members. This type of bookkeeping causes individuals to look for other means of getting to where they have to go in order to make the department's operation, relative to its budget, look good at the end of the fiscal period. A much better practice is to consider the aviation department or aircraft operating cost as part of the overall company overhead. This tends to encourage use of the aircraft which, in the long run, reduces the cost of operation relative to its utility.

Employees' Time and Productivity

One of the dollars and cents justifications most frequently cited in trying to prove the advantages of aircraft use is the saving of executive time. But how does one figure the value of a man's time? Should it be equal to the amount paid him in terms of salary and other benefits? Or is there a way to determine how much gross business each hour of his effort should be worth to the company? Some management-consultant types have come up with a formula which is useful for this purpose and hard to disprove. It is based on the generally accepted theory that any increase in salary and/or other benefits must be predicted on and accompanied by considerably greater increases an individual productivity.

Here is how that works. Assuming most salaried employees, whether executive or other, spend 2,000 hours a year on the job and are actually productively occupied only about 1,500 hours a year, a 2.5 percent productivity factor per each $10,000 of yearly salary is cranked in. This scaled up productivity factor determines the amount of value per hour to the company expected of each employee. Table 1-2 shows how this works out for employees and executivies, ranging in annual remuneration from $10,000 to $100,000. By multiplying the figures in the fourth column from the left by the number of hours which can be saved by the use of company aircraft, this time saving can be equated with a sensible dollar figure. In columns six and seven we have entered such arbitrary time savings and the associated dollar amounts against which the cost of aircraft ownership and operation can be compared.

If the figures representing the expected annual contribution of the individual to the company's gross business seem excessive at first glance, they do prove to be quite realistic when looked at in the context of a company's work force and gross business. To illustrate, let's look at Table 1-3. Here we show the number of employees in each salary bracket and the total contribution which they are expected to make to the company gross. In this sample the company would be reporting an annual gross business of $30,944,835, which is produced by a work force being paid total salaries of $7,275,000. Based on the annual reports of a large

Table 1-2. The Value of a Man's Time to the Company Which Employs Him.

Yearly salary	Hourly pay	Productivity factor	Contribution per hour to company	Annual contribution of the individual	Number of travelers	Hours saved	Gain in dollars
$ 10,000.00	$ 5.00	2.5	$ 12.50	$ 18,750.00	15	87	$ 1,087.50
15,000.00	7.50	3.75	28.13	42,195.00	23	133	3,741.29
20,000.00	10.00	5	50.00	75,000.00	34	218	10,900.00
30,000.00	15.00	7.5	112.50	168,750.00	27	178	20,025.00
40,000.00	20.00	10	200.00	300,000.00	9	114	22,800.00
50,000.00	25.00	12.5	312.50	468,750.00	5	212	66,250.00
75,000.00	37.50	18.75	703.13	914,695.00	3	199	139,922.87
100,000.00	50.00	25	1,250.00	1,875,000.00	1	78	97,500.00
							$459,726.66

Table 1-3. Dollar Contributions to the Company Gross Which Can Be Expected from Employees in Different Salary Brackets.

Yearly salary	number of employees	Expected annual contribution to gross
$ 10,000	200	$ 3,750,000
15,000	100	4,219,500
20,000	75	5,625,000
30,000	42	7,087,500
40,000	11	3,300,000
50,000	5	2,343,750
75,000	3	2,744,085
100,000	1	1,875,000
		$30,944,835

Total salaries: $7,275,000

number of different types of corporations, this relationship would seem to be right in the ball park.

In recent years most companies have found that there is less and less resistance by accountants and stockholders to the acceptance of aircraft as a legitimate business machine. Even the general public, including those who have never set foot in a non-airline aircraft and never expect to, has learned to accept the fact that personal and business aircraft are things other than rich men's toys. Much of the increased acceptance of business aircraft is the result of the fuel situation and the related reduction in airline schedules, coupled with the 55-mph speed limit on the nation's highways. Granted, the fuel situation has also increased the cost of aircraft use. But this increase is in no way comparable to the increase in wasted time when other means of transportation are being used.

Chapter 2
Own, Lease or Rent?

There are all kinds of ways to have aircraft available when they are needed, and all have their advantages and disadvantages in terms of cost as well as convenience. Basically they fall into three categories: outright purchase, long or short-term lease, and rental with or without a professional pilot, which would include the use of air charter services.

Purchase for Cash

Most companies and individuals, if their finances permit, will prefer to opt for an outright purchase. This means that the aircraft is always available when it is needed, and will, in the long run, also prove to be the most financially advantageous choice. The trouble is that the initial cost is considerable, even if the purchase is associated with a six or seven-year financing arrangement.

From a pure dollars and cents standpoint an outright purchase for cash is by far the best deal. It involves a huge initial outlay, which can amount to from under $50,000 for a used high performance single or a light twin to over $5 million for some of the top-of-the-line corporate jets. A purchase for cash eliminates the rather considerable cost of interest and leaves the owner free to choose whatever insurance coverage he feels he wants to buy. With interest rates being as high as they are these days, the cost of using other people's money has, on the surface at least, gone right through the roof. I say on the surface because with the present rate of inflation fluctuating around 12 percent a year an interest rate of 18 percent is, in fact, only six percent in real dollars. And if one is lucky enough to find someone who will lend money at 12 percent, the loan is actually for free.

Regardless of whether the aircraft is purchased for cash or on time, all expenses associated with the operation, maintenance and insurance of the aircraft are the responsibility of the owner. It is, of course, possible to have several individuals or companies jointly purchase an aircraft, which is then available to be used by each of the owners. Depending on the number of such partners, the initial as well as continuing expense is cut into two, three, four or more parts, but the availability of the aircraft to each of the various owners is also reduced by the same percentage. Usually, especially when ownership is divided among more than two entities, it will become necessary to employ someone who handles the scheduling in order to avoid conflicts and the resulting ill feeling.

Rental Services

Diametrically opposed to outright ownership is the alternative of using rental aircraft or charter services. Aircraft can be rented at just about any airport in the country. The standard rental arrangement calls for a so-called wet rate per hour, meaning that the rental fee includes gas and oil. The renter agrees to pay so many dollars per hour, usually including a two or three-hour minimum for each day the aircraft is kept away from home base. Upon presentation of the fuel and oil purchase receipts to the FBO (fixed base operator), he is reimbursed for those amounts.

Landing fees, tiedowns and the like are the responsibility of the renter, and the FBO takes care of all maintenance, insurance and so on. But it must be understood that the insurance carried by the FBO in most instances is only for his own protection and that of the renter. As a matter of fact, if a claim is made for some damage which has occurred while the aircraft was being flown by a renter pilot, the insurance company, after paying the claim to the FBO, is likely to turn around and try to recover the sum from the renter pilot, if necessary by filing suit. Several insurance companies offer relatively inexpensive renter-pilot policies which are designed to protect the renter. Anyone using rental aircraft with any degree of frequency would be well advised to buy such a policy.

Charter Services

If the person wishing to use a rental aircraft prefers not to do his own flying, he can hire a pilot. This can get a bit complicated. Most FBOs, in addition to renting airplanes, also operate charter services. But in most cases the fee charged for a charter is considerably higher than the wet rental of the aircraft, plus the hourly fee of the pilot. As a general rule, each FBO, who does a reasonable amount of charter business, has a fixed table of rates to frequently used destinations. It is always a good idea to compare these rates to what it would cost to simply rent the airplane and possibly employ the services of a flight instructor to do the actual flying. But this, too, can backfire.

Charter rates are fixed and do not increase if a strong headwind causes the trip to take longer than was expected. Rentals, on the other hand, are based on the actual time during which the engine runs. They tend to increase when adverse weather conditions result in increased tach time. Rental aircraft are nearly always equipped with so-called *Hobbs meters* which record the actual time in hours and tenths of hours from the time the main switch is turned on to the time it is turned off. It is therefore of no advantage to fly with a low rpm (revolutions per minute) setting which would reduce the time recorded on the tach, but not on the Hobbs meter.

The obvious advantage of renting or chartering is that all maintenance, hangaring and the other expensive nuisance associated with aircraft ownership is eliminated. A meaningful disadvantage is that one can never be absolutely certain that the aircraft is being maintained in tip top condition. The other pilots flying it have done so with the care and respect which a well-maintained airplane deserves. The other drawback is that the choice of available airplanes is usually limited to relatively low performance singles and light twins.

One unique charter-type service is offered by Executive Jet of Columbus, Ohio. Executive Jet (EJA), as it is generally known, operates a fleet of Learjets, Westwinds and other jet aircraft (fig. 2-1). Companies which subscribe to its service, usually by guaran-

Fig. 2-1. One of Executive Jet Aviation's fleet of Westwind turbojet aircraft.

teeing EJA a certain amount of use over a given period of time, can call the EJA 800-number at any time and arrange for their employees to be picked up at any place in the United States and to be flown to any other place. It isn't cheap, around $2 per mile. When the cost can be split between four or five people, though, it isn't too bad. Executive Jet issues a gold-plated credit card which is produced for it by Tiffany in new York. It is a great conversation piece, but presenting it will not get you a Learjet unless your current credit rating can be satisfactorily checked. Many companies with fleets of aircraft of their own will use EJA when there is a scheduling conflict and the trip is of sufficient importance.

Leasing

In between the outright purchase of an aircraft and the use of rental or charter services lies the lease alternative. A large number of companies specialize in leasing aircraft of all types, from the smallest singles to the most expensive executive jets. Some insist on long-term leases, five to eight years, while others are flexible and will lease aircraft for virtually any time period.

The average yearly lease expense comes to about 20 percent of the purchase price of the aircraft including all optional equipment. The advantage is that it eliminates the initial cash outlay involved with an outright purchase or the still large sum making up the down payment, though it may require an initial payment of the first and last month or two. Instead, the monthly or yearly cost remains the same throughout the life of the lease. Most long term leases include a clause by which the aircraft will become the property of the lessee at the conclusion of the lease and upon payment of an additional predetermined sum.

As a general rule, short-term leases are available only for the higher priced aircraft, usually entered into for the purpose of having an aircraft available while the company waits for the delivery of an aircraft which it has on order. These days the elapsed time between the data at which an order has been placed (an an initial payment made) for one of the new turboprops or jets and the date of actual delivery of the aircraft, comlete with the desired avionics package and custom interior, can run into several years. The short-term lease of a comparable aircraft can solve the company's transportation problem during that period.

Aware of the shortage of available top of the line aircraft relative to the demand, some leasing companies such as the Omni Trading Floor have been known to buy delivery positions from companies which had placed an order for a particular turboprop or jet but which, for some reason, decided against going through with the purchase. By doing this these companies are assured of a continuing supply of first class equipment available for lease or sale in the years to come.

Purchase Options and Delivery Positions

Purchase options and the associated delivery positions are an important consideration for the manufacturers who are in the process of developing, building and certificating a new type of aircraft. The development of a new jet, such as the *Canadair Challenger*, involves an investment in terms of risk capital of millions of dollars (Fig. 2-2). Virtually no company would go ahead and undertake such a project unless it was more or less assured of a certain number of sales. What happens is the company will advertise the new aircraft long before the initial metal cutting process starts. It will specify a delivery price for the aircraft which is going to be firm for the first dozen or two aircraft which will be delivered. After that the price is then likely to increase by the amount of inflation or even somewhat more. As a result companies will take the chance of placing a down payment on an as yet nonexistent aircraft in order to insure not only an early delivery date but also the lower price.

As an example, at this writing the Learfan, the revolutionary turboprop which was the last design by the late William P. Lear, is strictly a paper airplane. Construction of the prototype is still in the earliest stages at the LearAvia facility in Reno, and the company is

Fig. 2-2. The Canadair Challenger, one of three corporate jets with true intercontinental range.

negotiating with a number of major manufacturers in several countries for a manufacturing agreement, once the prototype has been certificated. But even at this early stage LearAvia reports having firm options for some two dozen planes.

An exception to this practice is the *Diamond I* business jet developed by Mitsubishi in Japan. Though there had been rumors for several years that such an aircraft was on the horizon, Mitsubishi built and tested the airplane in complete secrecy in Japan and only introduced it to the American public when a demonstrator was ready to be shown and certification was all but assured. At that point one aircraft was brought to the United States and purchase options were offered at a miniscule (for a $2 million aircraft) down payment of $75,000. A fair number of these were snapped up, some of them probably by companies who assumed it to be a safe gamble. Even if they should eventually decide that they didn't want the airplane, there would be plenty of takers for these early delivery positions.

Aviation Consultant Firms

A company may finally realize that its travel needs are being poorly served by the use of commercial airlines and the automobile, and that one or several company airplanes might just be what the doctor ordered. When there is no one in the upper management ranks in the company who is a pilot or otherwise knowledgeable in aviation matters, the question arises, whom do we turn to for advice? Obviously the major airframe manufacturers, their dealers and distributors, have a vested interest in being helpful. Each will necessarily attempt to sell its own aircraft without giving consideration to the fact that a competitor's model may be the better choice. For instance, a company with extensive short distance travel needs, say, 200-mile missions or less, when consulting one of the three major airframe companies, may find itself being sold some high-performance singles or light twins. In fact, its needs would be much better served by a helicopter (Fig. 2-3).

The trick, then, is to start out to get advice from someone who isn't trying to sell any hardware. There is a large number of so-called aviation consultant firms located in many of the major cities. Some of these, though by no means all, specialize in preparing detailed analyses of a company's transportation needs and of the advantages and costs associated with different types of aircraft which might be used to satisfy those needs more efficiently. Like

Fig. 2-3. Some company's travel needs are best served by a helicopter.

all management consultants, these people charge for their service. It is the only thing they have to sell. Considering the potentially high cost of getting started in company aviation on the wrong foot (or with the wrong pair of wings), this may just be a drop in the bucket. Most of these firms can be found in the World Aviation Directory (Ziff-Davis Publishing Company) under *consultants and special services*. The directory also lists all kinds of other types of services and only those which describe themselves as *aviation management consultants* or *transportation consultants* should be considered.

National Business Aircraft Association

When in doubt, it might be a good idea to contact the National Business Aircraft Association (NBAA) (1 Farragut Square South, Washington D.C. 20006. The telephone number is 202-783-9000). This organization publishes a considerable amount of helpful material for use by operators of business and corporate aircraft, and also might be able to suggest a reliable source for the kind of advice being sought. Later on, when a company aircraft has been acquired, the compnay should seriously consider joining the NBAA, which has proven to be the most important and effective voice in business aviation.

Once it has been established that the aircraft to be purchased is most likely one from a particular manufacturer, let that manufacturer prepare a complete feasibility study (see Chapter 18). Provide him with as much transportation-related information as you possibly can, as any analysis, in order to be meaningful, must be based on the largest possible amount of correct available data. The so-called "big three" among the airframe manufacturers, *Cessna, Beech* and *Piper*, have entire departments strictly for the purpose of preparing such feasiblity studies for potential aircraft buyers. Their service is free and without obligation, and usually includes expert advice on such complicated subjects as depreciation, tax advantages and so on.

Aviation Publications

Among the aviation publications, the only one which concentrates on the problems confronting the business and corporate flight operations is *Business and Commercial Aviation* (Ziff-Davis Publishing Company). Each issue contains carefully researched analyses of business aircraft, business aviation operations, avionics, etc. There are other publications in this field (*Professional Pilot, Flight Crew*, and for the helicopter operator, *Rotor and Wing*), but each of these is of more value after a company aviation operation has been established.

And while on the subject of publications, for the individual owner pilot there are *Flying, Aero* (distributed free to owners of all relatively new aircraft), and the *AOPA Pilot* (distributed to members of the Aircraft Owners and Pilots Association). There are a host of lesser publications aimed primarily at the private and sports pilot.

Aviation, when looked at as an activity designed to improve business effectiveness, is an extremely complex subject. A wrong purchase decision might be made because of a lack of understanding of what is involved or as a result of an emotional attachment to one kind of aircraft or manufacturer. For that matter, it might be made as the result of a highly effective though ill-conceived sales pitch. Anyway, it can easily prove to be a terribly expensive adventure resulting, in extreme cases, in the eventual abandonment of any aviation involvement, often to the detriment of the company. Any time and effort spent in advance evluation and research can only pay big dividends in the long run.

Chapter 3
The Airplanes

While virtually any kind of airplane can theoretically be used as a business machine, fixed-gear single-engine airplanes, except for a few high performance models, are usually not included in any evaluation of business aircraft. Those that do legitimately fall into the business aircraft category number nearly 100 fixed-wing models and over two dozen helicopters. It is not our purpose here to evaluate each and every model. Such evaluations, complete with all meaningful performance parameters, are available in the *The Illustrated Encyclopedia of General Aviation* (TAB book No. 2274), the annual fall and winter issues of *Flight Crew* magazine, and in the annual April *Planning and Purchasing Handbook* issue of *Business and Commercial Aviation* magazine.

What this chapter is trying to do is to give an evaluation of the advantages and disadvantages of the different categories of aircraft which are available for business use. In each evaluation we have used averages, meaning that some models will do better, while others will be below those averages in one parameter or another.

Single-Engine Aircraft

In this category there are 20 normally aspirated models, 10 turbocharged models, and one with pressurization (Fig. 3-l). Of these, two, the *Cessna Skywagon* models, have conventional fixed gear (taildraggers), seven have a tricycle fixed gear, and the balance have retractable gears. In terms of cost, adequately equipped to be used IFR (instrument flight rules) for business, they start at just under $60,000 and go up to $125,000 for the normally aspirated models, $135,000 for the turbocharged versions, and $160,000 for Cessna's *Pressurized Centurion* (Fig. 3-2).

Fig. 3-1. The Cessna Skywagon with its conventional gear is a favorite among pilots operating in undeveloped areas around the world.

But the cost of acquisition, though initially important should never be the primary deciding factor. Much more vital are the various parameters which influence the cost of operation and the different performance figures which may or may not reveal that the particular aircraft is suited for the kind of job expected of it.

Operating Costs

In terms of operating costs, the two primary data are the fuel consumed in order to go a given distance, and the time between major engine overhauls. The average fuel flow per hour at a reasonable power setting is 73 pounds (12.17 gallons) for the 20 normally aspirated models, 77.4 pounds (12.9 gallons) per hour for the turbocharged aircraft, and 88 pounds (14.67 gallons) per hour for the *Pressurized Centurion*. But the rate of fuel flow per hour is only meaningful if it is related to the speed of the aircraft, or the number of miles one can expect to travel in that hour. Here, the average cruise speed for the first group of 20 is 145.5 knots, for the turbocharged group it comes to 153.9 knots. The pressurized model cruises at 171 knots.

The simplest way to find out which airplane does best in terms of fuel and, in turn, cost per mile, is to deduct the fuel flow per hour figure from the speed (knots or mph) figure and see which one results in the highest total, indicating that the least fuel is used for the most miles. Among the first 20 aircraft, the ones which come out best in this exercise are the *Bellanca Aries T-250* and the *Mooney 201* (Fig. 3-3) The Aries goes 2.4 nautical miles (nm) on a pound of fuel, while the 201, though a somewhat slower airplane,

Fig. 3-2. The pressurized Centurion is rapidly becoming a favorite among business users of single-engine aircraft.

gets 2.7 nm per pound of fuel. On the other hand, both of these are four-seat airplanes while some in the group can seat six. Therefore, with a full load, the advantages would disappear in terms of passenger miles.

Among the turbocharged aircraft the *Mooney 231* wins hands down with 2.76 nm per pound of fuel, the next best being the *Rockwell Alpine Commander* (no longer in production) at 2.4 nm (Figs. 3-4 and 3-5). Again, both these aircraft have four seats, while there are others with six.

The lone pressurized model doesn't do too well in this category, with 1.94 nm per pound of fuel. It does have a seating capacity for six.

Fig. 3-3. The Mooney 201 is one of the most economical single-engine aircraft.

Fig. 3-4. The Mooney 231 with turbocharging is among the fastest single-engine aircraft.

There can be no question about the fact that, dollar for dollar, the various single-engine aircraft are by far the best deal available in aviation. They are not that much slower than many of the twins. They are easy to fly, and the costs of operation and maintenance are only slightly more than half those of their twin-engine counterparts. The primary drawback is exactly what makes them economical, the fact that there is only one engine. Reaction by both, pilots and non-pilots, varies to the idea of flying in an airplane with only one engine. Some, myself included, feel perfectly safe and comfortable. I will fly single-engine airplanes day or night, over land or water, without being the least bit bothered by the knowledge that if that one engine should decide to give me trouble, there's no place to go but down. Modern engines, when well maintained and cared for, don't just suddenly quit. If something should start to go wrong, there is virtually always some sort of advance warning, either in terms of engine sound or in the readings of the cylinder-head, oil-temperature, or exhaust-gas-temperature gauges.

On the other hand, business aircraft are often used to fly company personnel, customers and others. Even if the pilot is happy with just one engine, the passengers may not be. In that case aircraft ownership may defeat its purpose, and it would be better to opt for the added expense associated with multi-engine aircraft.

Multi-Engine Piston Aircraft

This group, too, is subdivided into a number of individual categories. There are the so-called owner-flown twins, either normally aspirated or turbocharged, with cabins seating either four or six, in a manner which means that once you're on the airplane and in your seat you stay put. Then there are those which are referred to as cabin-class aircraft, meaning that they have a (narrow) aisle which permits a degree of moving about in flight. All of those, currently on the market, are turbocharged. And then there are the pressurized models, some of the owner-flown type, some cabin-class. All in all there are 30 multi-engine models, 11 normally aspirated, six turbocharged owner-flown and five turbocharged cabin class, plus five pressurized owner-flown and three pressurized cabin class. (It must be understood that all pressurized models are turbocharged, as it is the turbocharger which provides the pressurization.)

Prices

Let's talk about prices of adequately equipped planes. In the normally aspirated group they range from just over $100,000 to close to $300,000, with three being four-seaters while all the rest seat six. The most expensive in the group, the *Rockwell Shrike Commander,* while normally considered in the owner-flown category, does have room to move around in flight (Figs. 3-6 and 3-7). The cockpit is more or less separated from the cabin itself, with a separate door for the pilot and the passengers. In the owner-flown turbocharged group, prices start at under $150,000 for the *Piper Seneca II* to over $250,000 for the *Beech Baron 58TC* (Figs. 3-8 and

Fig. 3-5. Another turbocharge single-engine aircraft, the Rockwell Alpine Commander.

Fig. 3-6. The Rockwell Shrike Commander is the only so-called owner-flown twin with a cabin which is large enough to permit getting up during flight.

3-9). In the turbocharged cabin-class group, the prices go from just under $300,000 to close to $400,000. While all turbocharged owner-flown aircraft have six seats, the cabin class ones range from seven to 10 seats. Among the pressurized airplanes, the owner-flown ones, all six-seaters, start at just under $200,000 and go up to over $400,000. The three cabin-class aircraft, all with seven seats, range from $345,000 to $450,000.

Fuel Statistics

The fuel flow for the normally aspirated models averages 133 pounds (22.17 gallons) per hour, with the average speed being

Fig. 3-7. A view of the cabin of the Rockwell Shrike Commander.

Fig. 3-8. The Piper Seneca II, one of the most popular turbocharged light twins.

173.5 knots. In the owner-flown turbocharged group the fuel flow averages 149 pounds (24.83 gallons) for a speed of 181.4 knots. By contrast, the turbocharged cabin-class twins use 189 pounds (31.5 gallons) of fuel, cruising at 184.4 knots. The figures for the owner-flown pressurized class are 179.4 pounds (29.9 gallons) versus 202.8 knots. The three cabin-class pressurized aircraft average 207.3 pounds (34.56 gallons) and 195.3 knots.

Looking at which one does best in the fuel-versus-miles traveled category in each group, we find among the normally aspirated twins with four seats, the *Gulfstream-American Cougar* beats all at 1.88 nm per pound of fuel. Among the six-seat models it's the *Piper Aerostar 600* at 1.34 nm per pound of fuel (Fig. 3-10). In the owner-flown turbocharged group, the Piper Seneca II gets 1.38 nm per pound, followed by both the *Cessna Turbo Skymaster* and the *Piper Aerostar 601* with 1.29 nm (Figs. 3-11 and 3-12).

Fig. 3-9. The turbocharged version of the Beech Baron 58.

Fig. 3-10. The Piper Aerostar, the fastest owner-flown piston twin in its class.

Among the turbocharged cabin-class twins it's the seven-seat *Piper Navajo,* with 1.11 nm per pound; the *Cessna Titan,* a 10-seat aircraft, brings up the rear with 0.8 nm per pound (Figs. 3-13 and 3-14). As far as the owner-flown pressurized airplanes are concerned, the *Pressurized Skymaster* leads with 1.34 nm, followed by the *Piper Aerostar 601P* with 1.31 nm (Figs. 3-15 and 3-16). In the cabin-class group the *Cessna Chancellor* wins with 1.06 nm (Fig. 3-17).

While the differentiation between owner-flown and cabin-class may imply that the latter needs to be flown by a professional crew, this is not the case. All aircraft talked about so far can be flown by any appropriately rated private (or commercial) pilot. Conversely, a company may decide to have any of these airplanes, including the singles, flown by a professional pilot (or even two), if that will help to increase the effective utilization of the airplanes.

Turboprop Aircraft

Now we leave the relatively uncomplicated area of the piston-engine airplanes and embark on the fields of turbines. Turboprop (or propjet) aircraft are powered by so-called turboshaft

Fig. 3-11. The Skymaster with turbocharged engines, one of the easiest to fly twins.

Fig. 3-12. The turbocharged version of the Aerostar.

engines in which the turbine drives a shaft to which a propeller is attached. These aircraft fly faster and higher than the piston-powered ones (though not much higher than the turbocharged pistons), but not as fast as the turbojets and fanjets. They use jet fuel in much greater quantities than pistons but, again, in lesser amounts than the jets. Though these aircraft, too, may be flown by any single appropriately rated private or commercial pilot, most business and corporate operations flying these aircraft employ a crew of two professional pilots on each airplane.

Seventeen different turboprop models are currently on the market. One, the *Learfan 2100*, may not actually start being delivered to customers for several years. The models range in price,

Fig. 3-13. The Piper Navajo, one of the most economical cabin-class twins.

Fig. 3-14. The huge Cessna Titan, the largest among the piston-powered cabin-class twins.

adequately equipped, from just under $700,000 up to $1,500,000. While most, in addition to a crew of two, can accommodate six to eight passengers, at least one, the *Swearingen Merlin IVA,* has room for up to 20 (Fig. 3-18).

All of these aircraft, with the single exception of the *Gulfstream-American Hustler,* have two engines. The Hustler is powered by one nose-mounted turboprop engine, plus one auxiliary pure jet engine which is mounted in the tail of the aircraft.

The fuel consumption for the group averages 464.2 pounds of jet fuel per hour (69.28 gallons). In the days when jet fuel was cheap, this didn't amount to much. Today, with the stuff selling at around $1.10 per gallon, fuel has become a major item for all turbine aircraft. In terms of speed, at the economy power setting for which the fuel flow was figured, they average 258.7 knots, the fastest being the *Mitsubishi Solitaire* with an economy cruise of 302

Fig. 3-15. The pressurized version of the easy to fly Cessna Skymaster.

Fig. 3-16. The pressurized Aerostar.

knots (Fig. 3-19). Looking at the number of nautical miles flown per pound of fuel used, the results are 0.55 nm average. The *Cessna Conquest* and the *Rockwell Executive I* and *II* are doing best with 0.7 nm per pound of fuel (Figs. 3-20 and 3-21).

Service Ceiling

One additional consideration which is important in this category is the *service ceiling*, in other words, the ability to fly above most of the severe weather. Service ceilings range from 24,850 feet for the *Beech King Air A100* to 41,000 feet for the Hustler and the (not yet certified) Learfan 2100, with most falling in the 28,000 to 32,000-foot range (Fig. 3-22). This means that, unlike the pure jets, these aircraft will have to detour around most thunderstorms instead of being able to safely fly over them. In addition, on

Fig. 3-17. Cessna's pressurized Chancellor.

Fig. 3-18. The commuter verson of the Merlin IV (in this version referred to as the Metro).

westerly flights, the usually strong westerly winds at those higher altitudes result in a considerably greater ground-speed reduction, percentage wise, than is the case with the jets.

Turbojet and Turbofan Aircraft

These are the pure jets, but the terms *turbojet* and *turbofan* require a bit of explanation. Originally all jet aircraft were pure

Fig. 3-19. The fastest among the turboprops, the Mitsubishi Solitaire.

Fig. 3-20. The latest entry in the turboprop competition, the Cessna Conquest.

jets, meaning that propulsion was the result of the thrust created by a stream of compressed air shooting out of the rear of the engines. These engines are most efficient at very high altitudes, where they are capable of developing very high speeds without gobbling up outrageous amounts of fuel. But at lower altitudes their fuel consumption climbs to incredible levels while efficiency is somewhat reduced. In addition they are incredibly noisy, and thus largely responsible for all that brouhaha about unacceptable airport noise.

Largely in order to deal with the fuel consumption and noise problems of these engines, the manufacturers developed the *fanjet* or *high bypass engine*. In these engines the compressed air is divided into two streams. One portion, the smaller one, shoots out

Fig. 3-21. One of the family of Rockwell International's turboprop aircraft.

Fig. 3-22. The Beech King Air A100, a popular corporate turboprop.

the back of the engines just as it does in the turbojets. But there is one important difference. Instead of rushing straight out, it spews in a circular ring of air around the outside of the center portion of the engine, thus creating a sort of invisible noise-canceling muffler. The major portion of the compressed air is used to drive a fan, much like a multi-bladed shrouded propeller, which greatly increases the speed with which the air is expelled to the rear, thus producing the major portion of the thrust. This is an over simplification. In actuality these engines are extremely complicated machines desipte the fact that they have fewer moving parts than piston engines. THat is why they cost as much as they do, and major overhauls can run up to $50,000 per engine.

All turbojet and turbofan aircraft, with the single exception of the *Citation I SP,* must be flown by a crew of two. This plane is the only one certificated for single-pilot operation and could, theoretically, be flown by any jet-rated private or commercial pilot. As a general rule, in corporate operations, all the aircraft are flown by air-transport rated captains with the aid of a copilot who has at least a commercial license with jet rating, and an instrument rating.

There are 19 models in this group, including one, the *Foxjet,* which may or may not ever see the light of day. Their prices, adequately equipped, range from a low of $750,000 for the yet iffy Foxjet or the more realistic $1,550,000 for the *Cessna Citation I,* to approximately $8,000,000 for the *Gulfstream-American Gulfstream III.* While all have a fairly respectable range, important because they must climb to altitude in order to effectively perform their missions, only four are truly intercontinental models. These are the Gulfstream II and III, the Canadair Challenger, and the

Fig. 3-23. A collection of Gulfstream IIs on one of the busier executive airports.

Dassault Falcon 50, the only one in the group with three engines (Figs. 3-23 and 3-24). All others have two.

Fuel Consumption

Looking at the fuel consumption figures, the average among all models (excluding the Foxjet) figures out to 1,620 pounds per hour average (241.8 gallons). The Cessna Citation I and II do best with 648 and 624 pounds (96.7 and 93.1 gallons) respectively. As far as cruise speed is concerned at power settings which use the fuel-flow figures listed, they average 402.6 knots. The Citation I is

Fig. 3-24. A head-on view of the intercontinental Canadair Challenger.

Fig. 3-25. Helicopters don't need airports for takeoffs and landing.

the slowest with 320 knots, and the Canadair Challenger 600 is the fastest at 460 knots.

Figuring the distances covered per pound of fuel burned, here is what we come up with: 0.29 nm per pound of fuel, average, with the Cessna Citation II doing best at 0.51 nm, and the Israel Aircraft Industries *Westwind I* at the bottom with 0.11 nm. Of the four intercontinental models the Canadair Challenger does best with 0.33 nm, followed by the Dassault Falcon 50 with 0.27 nm and the two Gulfstreams, II and III, with 0.14 and 0.17 nm respectively.

Helicopter Evaluation

The evaluation of helicopters is considerably more difficult than that of fixed-wing aircraft. The reason is that helicopters aren't bought for the same reasons, namely speed and range, as conventional aircraft. Helicopters are bought in order to carry people or freight over relatively short distances, distances for which speed is a minor consideration, without being restricted to using airports for takeoff or landing (Fig. 3-25). One type may be very slow, cruising at less than 100 knots, but capable of carrying incredible loads. Such machines are constantly used as aerial cranes in all manner of heavy construction projects. Others are small, seating maybe two or three, and capable of speeds in the 100 to 125-knot range. They are used for aerial surveillance, police work, rescue missions, fire fighting and 1,001 other jobs. Still others, somewhat larger, perform valuable service as aerial ambulances or people movers, cruising at speeds up to 140 or so knots.

And then there are the new so-called third generation type of helicopters, the twin-turbine executive ships which can carry six passengers (and a crew of two) in great luxury at speeds in excess of 150 knots over distances of 300 to 400 nm.

Helicopters, like most turbine-engine fixed-wing aircraft, are nearly always flown by professional crews. Helicopter flying looks a lot simpler than it is. It requires constant practice to remain proficient, something that cannot usually be expected of the average business or professional man.

Hovering Capability

Two performance parameters which are unique to the helicopter are its hovering capability in and out of ground effect (*HIGE* and *HOGE*). This refers to the ability of the helicopter to remain stationary at a given altitude above the terrain. It is always given in feet msl (mean sea level), which explains why the HIGE figure is always higher than the HOGE figure. In other words, if the terrain below is at a 10,000-foot elevation, the HIGE figure may be a given number of feet higher than that terrain figure. It would be impossible for the aircraft to hover at an altitude which would take it out of the terrain-related ground effect. This may not be particularly important for helicopters which are used exclusively for the transportation of persons or freight from one location to another. But if helicopters are to be used in such specialized tasks as rescue

Fig. 3-26. One of Enstrom's turbocharged piston helicopters.

Fig. 3-27. The IFR-certificated Bell Long Ranger, a single-turbine helicopter.

missions or construction projects in mountainous terrain, only those with a sufficiently high hovering capability can be used.

Helicopters come in three distinct groups. One group consists of those which are powered by piston engines, some turbocharged, most normally aspirated. The second group is powered by a single turbine engine, while the third group is powered by two turboshaft engines with the power from both translated into a combined powertrain which activates the main and tail rotors.

Piston-Powered Models

Currently there are eight piston-powered helicopters in production, two two-seaters, five three-seaters and one five-seater. Three of these, all manufactured by Enstrom, are turbocharged (Fig. 3-26). Prices, adequately equipped for the kind of flying for which they are designed, run from just under $45,000 up to $125,000. All cruise speeds in the 80 to 95-knot range (except for the *Hiller UH-12E* which has a top speed of 65 nm). The full-fuel range figures start at 181 nm for the *Robinson R22*, the lowest-priced model in the group, and go up to just under 300 nm for the *Hughes 300C*, a three-seat machine which has become a favorite of many big city police departments around the country. The HIGE numbers range from a low of 5,900 feet to a high of 15,500, with the normally aspirated models averaging 7,675 feet and the turbocharged models averaging 10,087 feet. In terms of feet HOGE, the low is 2,750 feet and the high 7,200 feet, with the normally aspirated models averaging 4,587 feet and the turbocharged models 8,800 feet.

Single Turbine Engine Models

The single-turbine-engine-helicopter group consists of eight models ranging in price, equipped, from around $250,000 to just under $1,000,000. Four are five-seaters, one seats six, one has seven seats, and the remaining two can accommodate 10, all including the crew. Cruising speeds range from 110 to 145 knots, with the *Aerospatiale Dauphin SA 360C* being the fastest. Full-fuel ranges average 316 nm, with at least one, the *Aerospatiale AStar,* being able to go 427 nm on full tanks. In the hovering category, the HIGE figures range from a high of 16,565 feet for the *Aerospatiale Lama* utility helicopter to a low of 5,575 for that same company's *Alouette III,* averaging 8,209 feet.

While none of the piston-powered helicopters are certificated to be flown under IFR conditions, an increasing number of turbine helicopters are being approved for IFR operations, some with one and others with two pilots. The prerequisite for such certification is always a fairly complicated and expensive instrument package, including a stability-augmentation system, the helicopter version of a sophisticated autopilot. This is a necessity for IFR flights as, without it, helicopters will not remain stable for even brief periods of time if the pilot takes his hands off the controls.

At this writing three of the single-turbine helicopter models are certificated for IFR operation, all requiring only a single pilot. They are the *Bell Long Ranger II,* the *Aerospatiale Dauphin* and the stretched *Gazelle* from that same company, which is also certificated for operation down to *CAT II* landings (Fig. 3-27).

Twin Turbine Models

The last group is comprised of the twin turbine helicopters. There are ten in that group, ranging in price from just under $1,000,000 to $3,750,000. No price is as yet available for the

Fig. 3-28. Boeing Vertol's giant twin-rotor Chinook.

Fig. 3-29. The Bell 222, a third generation twin-turbine executive helicopter.

passenger and utility versions of Boeing Vertol's giant twin-rotor *Chinook* (Fig. 3-28). Seating capacity varies all over the place, from five seats for the *Messerschmitt-Bolkow-Blohm Bo-105*, seven seats for the *Bell 222*, eight seats for the *Giovanni Agusta 109A* and the *Sikorsky S-76 Spirit*, ten seats for the Aerospatiale Daupin 2 and the *Bell 212*, 14 seats for the executive configuration of the *Aerospatiale Puma*, 22 seats for *Sikorsky's Mark II s-61N*, and 46 seats for the passenger version of the *Boeing Vertol Chinook*. In all instances these seat figures include the crew. All of these aircraft, except the Bo-105 and the Augusta 109A, are designed to be flown by a crew of two, with all being certificated for IFR operations (Figs. 3-29 through 3-32).

In terms of cruise speed, the performances vary from a high of 155 knots down to 100, the average being 134 knots. Full-fuel ranges are 740 nm for the Chinook and down to 230 for the Bell 212, but averaging 402 nm. The hovering capabilities average out to 10,078 feet for HIGE and 5,894 feet for HOGE.

Of this group, the ones being watched by the business community with the greatest interest are the three relatively new

Fig. 3-30. The Agusta 109A, a twin-turbine helicopter manufactured in Italy.

Fig. 3-31. The Sikorsky S-76 Spirit, another third generation twin-turbine executive helicopter.

additions, designed primarily as executive transports over distances averaging in the 300-nm range. They are the Bell 222, the Sikorsky S-76 Spirit, and the Aerospatiale Dauphin 2. All of these are making a concerted effort to be regarded as viable competition for cabin twins and turboprops.

To date the largest number of those delivered are being used by the offshore oil people in moving crews to and from the hundreds

Fig. 3-32. The twin-turbine Bell 212, one of the earliest twin-turbine helicopters.

Fig. 3-33. Chinook unloading passengers on an oil exploration platform in the Gulf of Mexico.

of drilling and production platforms (Fig. 3-33). These users, who need to transport personnel by the tens of thousands each month to locations which can practically only be served by helicopters, are anxiously awaiting the beginning of customer deliveries of the Chinook. It is generally hoped the Chinook will be the forerunner of even bigger machines, capable of moving between 100 and 200 passengers. The British, with all that oil exploration activity in the North Sea, have repeatedly expressed an urgent need for such giant aircraft.

Chapter 4

One Engine or Two?

Let's face it. There is nothing quite as reassuring for the ego of a businessman/pilot flying his own light aircraft as a fistful of throttles controlling two engines, rakishly cantilevered forward of each wing (Fig. 4-1). It produces a feeling of power and superiority that no single-engine airplane, no matter how sophisticated, can quite match.

And there is more to it. Passengers, accustomed to huge aerial whales with three power-spewing holes in the tail or four under the wings, feel more reassured by the illusion of added safety that is produced by engine redundancy. And, after all, much that is written about aviation deals with the idea that there is safety in numbers, especially when flying at night, IFR, or over water and hostile terrain.

Granted, the Federal Aviation Administration's (FAA) annual accident statistics do little to strengthen the validity of the claim of twin-engine safety. But then we always believe that they are talking about the other guy, the one who, unlike ourselves, is prone to commit some pilot error.

Let's examine the real value of that second engine with relation to the three parameters that are of primary importance to the pilot/owner: cost, performance and safety.

Cost Factor

The cost factor breaks down into three categories: the price of the aircraft, the cost of fuel and oil needed to operate it and the expense involved in maintenance and reserves for overhauls, hangar usage, insurance and so on. The performance parameters of primary interest are range, rate of climb, ceiling, payload capacity

Fig. 4-1. Two engines rakishly cantilevered forward of each wing, as in the Beech Duke.

and, of course, speed. And safety, well, all of today's airplanes are basically safe machines, assuming a fully competent pilot.

Single-engine aircraft with at least four seats which may be considered adequate for business use, range in price from $35,000 to $157,500. They are adequately equipped for the type of airplane and for the kind of flying for which most businessmen must be prepared. By comparison, piston twins start at $110,000, comparably equipped, piston twins start at $110,000, comparably equipped, and go all the way up to $411,000. Under no wind conditions the fuel efficiency of the singles, combined with reserve for overhaul, insurance, hangar usage and other expenses, ranges from 14 cents per nm to 26 cents per nm, while the same figures for twins are 24 cents to 49 cents.

Maintenance and Performance

As far as maintenance is concerned, twins are somewhat more than twice as costly to keep up. In addition to the second engine, more complicated systems require frequent additional attention (Fig. 4-2).

In the area of performance the differences are less startling. Using recommended economy power settings, the range figures for the singles go from 588 nm to 1,170 nm and for the twins from 730 to 1,818 n. The rate of climb is adequate for both, the singles and twins, except that in the case of twins some of the single-engine rate-of-climb figures are so low as to be relatively meaningless in practice. The same can be said for the service ceilings. Payloads, meaning the weight which can be carried with full fuel (in the case of cabin-class twins, excluding the weight of a professional pilot and his baggage and equipment, figured at 200 pounds) range from 432 to 1,127 pounds for the singles and from 571 to 1,336 pounds for the twins. And then there is speed, the performance figure which most pilots like to look at first and which most manufacturers feature most prominently in their advertising. In high-speed cruise, usually at 75 percent of power, the singles move along at from 127 to 200 knots, while the twins true out at from 160 to 257 knots. Using more realistic economy-cruise figures, they are from 103 to 174 knots and from 151 to 218 knots respectively.

The fact is that speed is a highly overrated performance parameter. Most of us find that we tend to be willing to pay all kinds of extra money in order to go a few knots faster. In fact, over distances of 500 nm or less, the difference in time aloft is too small to be anything to worry about.

Safety Factor

The safety factor is one which cannot be measured in numbers or illustrated in comparison charts. There can be no doubt that the

Fig. 4-2. Twin-engine aircraft maintenance costs are about twice those of the singles.

ability to keep flying in the event of an engine failure or malfunction adds meassurably to the safety of pilot and passengers. But this is where we often get into trouble. It does so only if the pilot is proficient at the emergency single-engine procedures applicable to his aircraft, and if he is aware of the performance limitations with one engine inoperative.

For example, too many multi-engine rated pilots forget that the single-engine climb capability of many of the non-turbocharged light twins is virtually nonexistent under all but the most ideal conditions. The FAA regulations do not require that a light twin be capable of demonstrated climb capability on one engine at gross. Therefore, an engine failure on takeoff on a warm day, or at an airport located at a several-thousand-foot elevation, in a twin can be considerably more hair raising than it would be in a single. A single-engine plane simply turns into a straight-forward glider instead of some asymmetrical beast that wants to neither glide straight ahead nor keep flying sufficiently to permit a safe turn back to the airport for landing. Similarly, the single-engine service ceiling of some non-turbocharged twins is below most IFR minimum enroute altitudes and, in mountain country, often below safe terrain clearance levels.

Based on these facts it might be stated with conviction that, in the hands of a professional or highly proficient non-professional pilot, the second engine does offer a measurable degree of added safety. But the average pilot who uses his aircraft for business cannot possibly be expected to maintain that highest degree of proficiency. He simply doesn't have the time to devote to practice left over from that needed to take care of his business and make a living.

Therefore, the businessman pilot, faced with the need to make a purchase decision between a high performance single and a light-twin, should put the multi-engine safety consideration on the bottom of the list of factors that will influence his choice. An examination of the cost versus the degree of utility relative to his individual needs should be the overriding yardstick.

It should be pointed out here that the center line-thrust twins, the three models of the Cessna Skymaster and the not yet in production *Rutan Defiant*, do combine the best of both worlds (Fig. 4-3). They offer that added degree of safety that comes with the second engine, while, even under single-engine conditions, being as easy to fly as any single-engine aircraft. The trouble with the models is that they don't "look like a twin" and that, as a result,

Fig. 4-3. Cessna's center-thrust Skymaster.

they don't offer that status symbol or ego building prestige thing that makes pilots long for an engine on each wing.

Chart Explanations

Tables 4-1 and 4-2 list the more meaningful cost and performance figures for 38 single-engine aircraft with four or more seats, and for 29 piston twins. Here is a detailed explanation of what to look for in these charts.

■ **Column 1.** The name of the manufacturer of the aircraft. We have included the single-engine aircraft manufactured by Rockwell International and by Gulfstream American even though, at this writing, both these companies have decided to stop manufacturing the singles. In each case the single-engine line, and, in the case of Gulfstream American the light twin, are for sale. It may be assumed that another company will continue to manufacture these aircraft. Abbreviations, used for space reasons, are BEE(Beech), BEL(Bellanca), CES(Cessna), GRA(Grumman American), MOO(Mooney), PIP(Piper), RIN(Rockwell International), but RUT (Burt Rutan). The Burt Rutan aircraft is not yet in production, but is included in the hopes that it will be in production by the time this book is in print).

■ **Column 2.** The model designation of the individual aircraft.

■ **Column 3.** The manufacturer's suggested retail price in 1979 dollars. This figure includes only standard equipment.

■ **Column 4.** The cost of the airplane fully equipped with avionics and other equipment needed to make full use of the

55

Table 4-1. Comparison Chart for Single-Engine Aircraft.

1 Manufacturer	2 Model designation	3 Suggested base price, 1979 $s	4 Estimated cost fully equipped, 1979 $s	5 Seats	6 Payload with full fuel, lbs	7 Range high-speed cruise, nm	8 Range economy cruise, nm	9 Max cruise speed, knots	10 Economy cruise speed, knots	11/12 Service ceiling, feet
PIP	Warrior II	24,040	35,000	4	693	520	635	127	103	14,000
PIP	Archer II	29,710	40,100	4	1050	515	670	131	107	15,000
GRA	Cheetah	30,900	40,100	4	528	657	734	127	104	12,600
CES	Skyhawk	33,150	39,950	4	583	630	750	122	115	14,200
MOO	Ranger	35,325	44,500	4	738	654	816	143	123	16,500
BEE	Sundowner	35,750	47,300	4	633	533	597	123	98	12,600
GRA	Tiger	37,000	46,900	4	692	554	588	139	118	13,800
PIP	Dakota	39,910	59,700	4	935	623	795	144	130	17,500
CES	Hawk XP	41,150	50,050	4	593	675	815	130	116	17,000
PIP	Arrow IV	44,510	69,800	4	725	810	875	143	131	17,000
MOO	201	46,725	68,900	4	716	835	929	169	152	18,800
CES	180 Skywagon	47,850	59,000	6	612	825	1010	142	124	17,700
BEE	Sierra	49,000	77,000	6	720	646	686	137	115	15,358
PIP	Turbo Arrow IV	49,150	74,300	4	800	675	860	172	154	20,000
CES	Skylane	49,645	59,700	4	718	880	1095	144	127	16,500
MOO	231	51,975	77,500	4	668	950	1135	183	163	24,000
PIP	Cherokee Six 300	52,030	79,000	7	975	679	835	152	132	17,100
CES	185 Skywagon	55,550	66,600	6	1127	680	835	145	129	17,150
BEL	Super Viking 17-30A	56,900	83,300	4	732	826	930	176	170	20,000
BEL	Aries T-250	60,000	82,000	4	844	990	1170	181	174	18,100
CES	Skylane RG	62,545	72,500	4	801	890	1135	156	139	18,000
CES	Stationair 6	63,235	75,500	6	432	725	900	147	130	14,800
PIP	Lance II	64,060	92,000	6	1068	656	714	158	139	15,400
CES	Turbo Skylane RG	68,550	79,400	4	661	875	988	173	147	20,000
CES	Turbo Stationair 6	69,895	81,500	7	918	690	785	167	NA	27,000
BEL	Super Viking 17-31ATC	70,380	96,250	4	645	666	695	193	144	24,000
PIP	Turbo Lance II	71,760	102,100	6	971	597	623	176	142	20,000
CES	Stationair 7	72,935	81,000	7	1142	565	690	143	126	13,300
CES	Centurion	79,845	90,000	6	1000	855	1065	171	154	17,300
CES	Turbo Stationair 7	79,910	91,100	7	1028	525	610	161	NA	26,000
BEE	Bonanza F33A	83,434	115,100	5	855	716	838	172	157	17,858
CES	Turbo Centurion	86,725	98,500	6	1118	815	940	196	NA	27,000
BEE	Bonanza V35B	89,284	117,000	5	874	716	838	172	157	17,858
BEE	Bonanza A36	89,284	117,000	6	1007	697	790	168	150	16,600
RIN	Alpine 112TCA	91,900	92,400	4	519	664	901	163	139	20,000
RIN	Gran Tourismo 114A	95,010	95,010	4	762	643	730	165	137	14,300
BEE	Bonanza A36TC	100,084	135,000	6	960	635	730	175	170	25,000
CES	Pressurized Centurion	117,030	157,500	6	864	770	925	200	NA	23,000

13/14 Rate of climb, fpm	15 Fuel capacity, lbs	16 Fuel flow, high speed, pph	17 Fuel flow, economy, pph	18 Turbocharged	19 Pressure differential, psi	20 TBO, hours	21 500-nm mission, hours:min	22 500-nm mission, fuel used, lbs	23 500-nm mission, fuel cost $1.20 gal	24 500-nm mission, reserves	25 500-nm mission, fuel + reserves	26 Cost per nm	27 500-nm mission, total cost incl. $20 per hour for one person	28 500-nm mission, total cost incl. $50 per hour for one person
710	288	60	40	—	—	2,000	4:54	194	38.83	39.20	78.03	.16	176.03	323.03
735	288	63	38	—	—	2,000	4:42	178	35.51	40.00	75.51	.15	169.51	310.51
660	316	51	37	—	—	2,000	4:48	178	35.58	40.85	76.43	.15	172.43	316.43
770	300	59	42	—	—	2,000	4:18	183	36.52	36.53	73.05	.15	159.05	288.05
800	312	56	42	—	—	2,000	4:00	171	34.15	35.80	69.95	.14	149.95	269.95
792	342	65	48	—	—	2,00	5:06	245	48.98	47.07	96.05	.19	198.05	351.05
850	316	64	51	—	—	2,000	4:12	216	43.22	38.60	81.82	.16	165.82	291.82
1110	432	82	56	—	—	2,000	3:48	215	43.08	39.79	82.87	.17	158.87	272.87
870	396	80	48	—	—	1,500	4:18	207	41.38	44.45	85.83	.17	171.83	300.83
831	432	71	48	—	—	1,600	3:48	183	36.64	46.00	82.64	.17	158.64	272.64
1030	384	65	52	—	—	1,600	3:18	171	34.21	39.65	73.86	.15	139.86	238.86
1100	504	85	55	—	—	1,500	4:00	222	44.35	44.93	89.28	.18	169.28	289.28
927	342	65	48	—	—	1,600	4:18	209	41.74	55.15	96.89	.19	182.89	311.89
940	462	84	55	TC	—	1,400	3:12	179	35.71	41.60	77.31	.15	141.31	237.31
1010	528	85	55	—	—	1,500	3:54	217	43.31	44.08	87.39	.17	165.39	282.39
1080	432	68	50	TC	—	1,400	3:06	153	30.67	41.30	71.97	14	133.97	226.97
1050	588	108	71	—	—	2,000	3:48	269	53.79	47.12	100.91	.20	176.91	290.91
1010	504	107	68	—	—	1,500	3:54	264	52.71	46.77	99.48	.20	177.48	294.48
1210	408	96	71	—	—	1,500	2:54	209	41.76	39.62	81.38	.16	139.38	226.38
1240	456	84	72	—	—	2,000	2:54	207	41.38	36.83	78.21	.16	136.21	223.21
1140	528	91	59	—	—	2,000	3:36	212	42.45	42.30	84.75	.17	156.75	261.75
920	528	106	68	—	—	1,500	3:48	262	52.31	48.96	101.27	.20	177.27	291.27
1000	564	108	71	—	—	2,000	3:36	255	51.08	49.32	100.40	.20	172.40	280.40
1040	528	86	64	TC	—	1,800	3:24	218	43.54	34.74	78.28	.16	146.28	248.28
1010	528	120	72	TC	—	1,400	3:00	216	43.11	41.16	84.27	.17	144.27	234.27
1170	408	95	70	TC	—	2,000	3:30	243	48.61	49.44	98.05	.20	168.05	273.05
1050	564	131	83	TC	—	1,800	3:30	292	58.45	42.74	101.19	.20	171.19	276.19
810	438	116	77	—	—	1,500	4:00	306	61.11	40.40	101.51	.20	181.51	301.51
950	534	105	68	—	—	1,500	3:12	221	44.16	45.87	90.03	.18	154.03	250.03
885	438	135	83	TC	—	1,400	3:06	419	83.85	45.51	129.36	.26	191.36	284.36
1167	444	91	69	—	—	1,500	3:12	220	43.95	53.90	97.85	.20	161.85	257.85
930	534	121	58	TC	—	1,400	2:36	308	61.73	40.10	101.83	.20	153.83	231.83
1167	444	91	69	—	—	1,500	3:12	220	43.95	54.51	98.46	.20	162.46	258.46
1030	444	91	69	—	—	1,500	3:18	230	46.00	56.21	102.21	.20	168.21	267.21
978	408	79	51	TC	—	1,600	3:36	183	36.69	51.71	88.40	.18	160.40	268.40
1037	408	89	66	—	—	2,000	3:36	241	48.18	50.40	98.58	.20	170.58	278.58
1165	444	101	74	TC	—	1,400	2:54	218	43.53	55.31	98.84	.20	156.84	243.84
930	534	130	75	TC	3.35	1,400	2:30	325	66.00	53.30	119.30	.24	169.60	244.30

airplane under VFR (visual flight rules) as well as IFR conditions. This figure is an estimate and can vary considerably, depending on the type and quality of the avionics and on individual equipment requirements.

■ **Column 5.** The seating capacity of the aircraft. This figure includes the pilot's seat.

■ **Column 6.** The payload with full fuel. For all practical purposes this is the useful load minus the fuel capacity, assuming long-range tanks where they are available, and, in the case of cabin-class twins, minus 200 pounds for the professional pilot and his equipment. In many instances aircraft can carry greater payload at the expense of some of the fuel and, in turn, of range.

■ **Columns 7 and 8.** There are range figures in nm, assuming a 45-minute reserve. They are based on full fuel, using long-range tanks where available. Column 7 shows the range at the recommended high speed cruise power setting, usually 75 percent. Column 8 shows the range which can be obtained by flying at economy cruise, usually 55 percent.

■ **Columns 9 and 10.** True airspeed in knots. Again, Column 9 shows the speed at the recommended high power setting, and Column 10 gives the figures for economy cruise.

■ **Columns 11 and 12.** Service ceiling is the altitude at which an aircraft will still climb at 100 feet per minute (fpm). Column 11 shows this figure for two engines and Column 12 for one engine. For this reason, the two columns are combined in the single-engine chart.

■ **Columns 13 and 14.** Rate of climb in fpm. Again, Column 13 shows the rate of climb for two engines and Column 14 for one engine, and in the single-engine chart the columns are combined. These figures are based on operation at sea level on a standard day (59 degrees Fahrenheit), at gross.

■ **Column 15.** Fuel capacity shown in pounds. Where long-range tanks are available, they are assumed to be installed in the aircraft. Anyone planning to use an aircraft in business should always opt for all the fuel capacity available.

■ **Columns 16 and 17.** Total fuel flow in pounds per hour. Column 16 gives this figure for high-speed cruise and Column 17 lists it for economy cruise. In the twin chart the figures represent the amount of fuel burned by both engines.

■ **Column 18.** The abbreviation TC indicates that the aircraft is turbocharged.

■ **Column 19.** These figures show the pressure differential in pounds per square inch (psi) for the pressurized aircraft.

■ **Column 20.** The time between overhauls recommended by the engine manufacturer, in hours.

■ **Columns 21 and 22.** In these and the subsequent columns we analyze a typical 500-nm mission. No allowance has been made for warm up or taxi time. Column 21 shows the time in hours and minutes which it takes the aircraft to cover the 500 nm at economy cruise, except in those few instances where figures for economy cruise were not available. There high-speed cruise was used. Column 22 shows the amount of fuel which was burned, in pounds.

■ **Column 23.** Here we show the fuel cost, based on a price of $1.20 per gallon.

■ **Column 24.** This figure represents the reserve for the major overhaul, a portion of the annual cost of insurance and of hangar usage and miscellaneous. Since these costs can vary considerably, we have taken the following arbitrary assumptions. We have figured the cost of a major overhaul per engine at $5,000. The insurance rate is calculated at 5 percent of the cost of the equipped aircraft, per year. Hangar fees and miscellaneous expenses were figured at $1,000 per year. The proportions allocated to the time it takes the aircraft to cover the 500-num distance is based on the assumption that the airplane is being flown 500 hours a year. Thus, taking the example of the *Cessna Skyhawk*, for instance, the major overhaul would be $5,000. The time between overhauls is 2,000 hours, which means that for each hour there must be a reserve of $2.50. It takes the Skyhawk 4.3 hours (four hours and 18 minutes) to cover the distance; therefore the reserve will amount to 2.5 times 4.3 equals $10.75. The insurance for the year would come to five percent of $39,950 or $1,997.50. With the airplane being flown 500 hours a year, that comes to $4 times the time en route, 4.3 equals $17.20. The hangar usage and miscellaneous figure of $1,000 per year amounts to $2 per hour or $8.60 for the trip. Thus the total fixed costs amount to $10.75 plus 17.20 plus 8.60 or $36.55. You will notice that in Table 4-1 the total is shown as $36.53 which resulted from the fact that here, in the example, we rounded off some of the fractions.

■ **Column 25.** This column shows the total cost of the trip, adding the cost of the fuel to the fixed costs.

■ **Column 26.** This is the cost per nautical mile, arrived at by dividing the total cost by 500.

Table 4-2. Comparison Chart for Twin-Engine Aircraft.

1 Manufacturer	2 Model designation	3 Suggested base price, 1979 $s	4 Estimated cost fully equipped, 1979 $s	5 Seats	6 Payload with full fuel, lbs	7 Range high-speed cruise, nm	8 Range economy cruise, nm	9 Max cruise speed, knots	10 Economy cruise speed, knots	11 Service ceiling, 2 engines, feet	12 Service ceiling, 1 engine, feet
PIP	Seminole	82,590	113,500	4	734	690	730	166	153	17,100	4,100
GRA	Cougar	86,120	110,000	4	519	840	1170	160	109	17,400	4,250
BEE	Duchess 76	91,850	125,500	4	870	623	780	166	151	19,650	6,170
PIP	Seneca II	102,530	146,700	6	954	783	882	190	165	25,000	13,400
CES	Skymaster	110,600	128,800	6	817	990	1235	169	149	16,300	6,900
CES	Turbo Skymaster	125,600	148,500	6	742	975	1125	200	NA	20,000	16,500
BEE	Baron B55	128,850	178,200	6	1079	798	991	188	173	19,300	6,400
PIP	Aztec F	130,810	173,500	6	916	1060	1320	179	170	17,600	4,800
PIP	Turbo Aztec F	151,615	196,000	6	779	947	1145	210	193	24,000	17,000
BEE	Baron E55	157,850	195,700	6	1063	993	1135	200	184	19,100	6,600
CES	310	159,990	180,000	6	714	884	1152	195	182	19,750	7,400
CES	Pressurized Skymaster	161,750	198,350	6	665	985	1155	205	179	20,000	18,700
BEE	Baron 58	183,750	236,200	6	907	1108	1339	200	184	18,600	7,000
PIP	Aerostar 600A	184,910	218,500	6	673	1103	1320	220	200	21,200	6,150
CES	Turbo 310	184,990	204,200	6	594	1240	NA	220	191	27,400	17,200
BEE	Baron 58TC	206,605	260,500	6	1312	958	1217	232	194	25,00	13,490
PIP	Aerostar 601B	211,150	242,200	6	968	1063	1244	257	218	30,000	9,300
PIP	Navajo	214,590	303,000	7	722	1005	1065	215	186	26,300	15,200
PIP	Navajo C/R	228,500	317,000	7	630	940	1040	220	180	26,400	15,300
CES	340	242,490	296,000	6	571	899	1036	229	NA	29,800	15,800
PIP	Chieftain	246,260	336,200	8	987	885	950	221	177	27,200	13,700
BEE	Baron 58P	250,000	337,500	6	1101	1008	1229	244	202	25,000	13,490
CES	402 Businessliner	263,990	296,000	6	1325	711	836	213	179	26,900	14,800
PIP	Aerostar 601P	265,280	310,100	6	706	1086	1271	257	209	25,000	9,300
CES	Chancellor	306,240	369,700	8	797	1147	1286	224	NA	31,350	19,800
BEE	Duke B60	313,000	411,000	6	1044	1072	1168	233	217	30,000	15,100
CES	Titan	345,490	384,600	10	1336	1406	1818	217	NA	26,000	10,100
CES	Golden Eagle	369,240	443,400	7	949	955	1092	241	NA	30,200	14,900
RUT	Defiant	NA	NA	4	890	930	1080	201	189	27,000	10,300

■ Columns 27 and 28. In these columns we have given the time spent en route two different dollar values. In Column 27 we have figured our time at $20 per hour and added that to the actual cost of the trip. In Column 28 we have figured our time at $50 and added that to the cost. The resultant figures prove that, if we value our time, the airplane with the lowest cost figure is not necessarily the most economical to use. The higher we figure our own value in terms of time, the greater is the influence of the time spent en route on the theoretical economy of the aircraft. In the case of the singles the turbocharged *Mooney 231* came out best in the $20-per-hour column and the *Bellance Aries T-250* in the $50-per-hour column. The *Piper Seminole* did best in the $20-per-hour column,

Rate of climb, 2 engines, fpm	Rate of climb, 1 engine, fpm	Fuel capacity, lbs	Fuel flow, high speed, pph	Fuel flow, economy, pph	Turbocharged	Pressure differential, psi	TBO, hours	500-nm mission, hours:min	500-nm mission, fuel used, lbs	500-nm mission, fuel cost $1.20 gal	500-nm mission, reserves	500-nm mission, fuel + reserves	Cost per nm	500-nm mission, total cost incl. $20 per hour for one person	500-nm mission, total cost incl. $50 per hour for one person
13	14	15	16	17	18	19	20	21	22	23	24	25	26	27	28
1340	217	660	134	89	—	—	2,000	3:18	290	58.08	60.56	118.64	.24	184.04	283.14
1160	200	708	133	67	—	—	2,000	4:36	307	61.46	82.80	144.26	.29	236.26	374.26
1248	235	600	136	93	—	—	2,000	3:18	308	61.59	64.52	126.11	.25	192.11	291.11
1340	225	768	142	108	TC	—	1,400	3:02	327	65.45	71.44	136.89	.27	197.49	288.39
940	300	888	160	106	—	—	1,500	3:22	356	71.14	73.26	144.40	.29	211.60	312.40
1160	335	888	174	120	TC	—	1,400	2:30	435	87.00	59.98	146.98	.29	196.98	271.98
1693	397	816	164	120	—	—	1,500	2:54	347	69.36	74.81	144.17	.29	202.17	289.17
1400	235	1063	144	106	—	—	1,600	2:56	312	62.35	74.24	136.59	.27	195.39	283.59
1470	225	1063	154	126	TC	—	1,400	2:35	326	65.28	74.73	140.01	.28	191.81	269.51
1682	398	996	186	138	—	—	1,500	2:42	375	75.00	76.24	151.24	.30	205.24	286.24
1662	370	1218	229	146	—	—	1,500	2:45	401	80.22	74.67	154.89	.31	209.89	292.39
1170	375	88	178	127	TC	3.35	1,400	2:47	355	70.95	80.54	151.49	.30	207.29	290.99
1660	390	1164	186	138	—	—	1,500	2:42	375	75.00	87.17	162.17	.32	216.17	297.17
1800	450	1047	NA	136	—	—	2,000	2:30	340	68.00	72.13	140.13	.28	190.13	265.13
1700	390	1218	376	298	TC	—	1,400	2:37	780	156.02	76.86	232.88	.47	285.28	363.88
1418	270	1140	230	148	TC	—	1,400	2:36	381	76.29	91.50	167.79	.34	219.79	297.79
1530	254	1047	164	144	TC	—	1,800	2:17	330	66.06	73.08	139.14	.28	184.94	253.64
1443	245	1124	NA	144	TC	—	1,800	2:41	387	77.42	102.21	179.63	.36	233.43	314.13
1500	255	1124	NA	144	TC	—	1,800	2:47	400	80.00	109.92	189.92	.38	245.52	328.92
1650	315	1218	258	205	TC	4.2	1,400	2:11	563	112.66	83.65	196.31	.39	239.91	305.31
1390	230	1124	NA	144	TC	—	1,800	2:49	406	81.36	115.29	196.65	.39	253.05	337.65
1418	270	1140	222	149	TC	3.9	1,400	2:30	369	73.76	107.23	180.99	.36	230.99	305.99
1450	301	1224	275	189	TC	—	1,400	2:47	528	105.59	108.48	214.07	.43	269.87	353.57
1530	254	1047	168	143	TC	4.25	1,800	2:23	342	68.42	92.56	160.98	.32	186.94	280.48
1580	290	1224	238	194	TC	5.0	1,400	2:14	531	106.25	101.45	207.70	.42	252.30	319.20
1601	307	1392	247	210	TC	4.6	1,600	2:18	484	96.77	115.98	212.75	.43	258.75	327.75
1575	230	2064	283	185	TC	—	1,200	2:18	652	130.41	112.22	242.63	.49	288.63	357.63
1940	350	1236	294	219	TC	5.0	1,200	2:06	610	121.99	114.81	236.80	.47	278.80	341.80
1850	580	660	115	93	—	—	2,000	2:36	246	49.21	NA	NA	NA	NA	NA

and in the $50-per-hour column the turbocharged *Piper Aerostar 601B* took the honors.

Applying Chart Figures

Throughout Tables 4-1 and 4-2 in those columns in which comparison is of consequence, we have emphasized the airplane(s) with the best parameters in a particular category by shading, in order to simplify the task of making some sort of sense out of that profusion of figures. A potential purchaser should be able to relate the figures in these charts to his average utilization in terms of usual trip lengths, payloads to be moved, and total hours to be

61

Fig. 4-4. Cessna's pressurized 340.

flown each year. This is done to arrive at the type of aircraft most suited to his particular requirements. And while at it, he should consider how often it might be necessary to carry people who may be put off by the idea of trusting their lives to a single engine. The percentage of hours likely to be flown in hard IFR conditions where an engine malfunction in a single-engine aircraft could easily become catastrophic. This, then, should be cranked into the decision making process when the question of single versus twin is being considered.

In the final analysis, of course, it quite often ends up being a question of dollars and cents. If the money for the initial investments is available and the projected use of the aircraft warrants the additional cost of operation, maintenance, insurance, hangar usage, landing fees and so on, then the decision will more than likely turn toward a multi-engine aircraft.

Pressurization

It might be a good idea to keep in mind the advantages of pressurization, now that Cessna, at least, is offering one single-engine and several not too expensive twins with pressurization (Fig. 4-4). Rumor has it that before long there'll be a pressurized Bonanza and, more probably than not, a pressurized Lance (Fig. 4-5 and 4-6).

All pressurized airplanes are, of course, turbocharged which, in the case of twins, means that the single-engine performance in terms of climb capability and service ceiling is greatly improved.

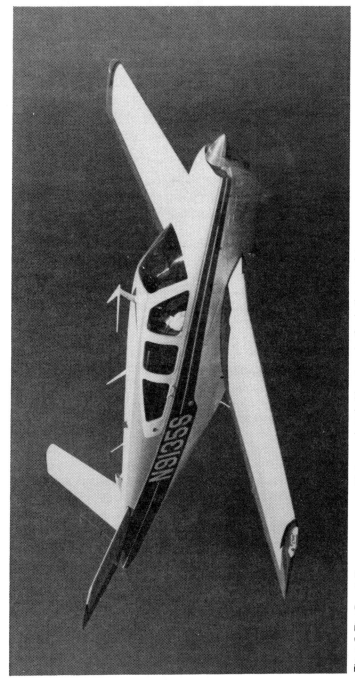

Fig. 4-5. The Beech Bonanza can expect to be produced with pressurization in the near future.

Fig. 4-6. The Piper Turbo Lance can be expected to hit the market with pressurization one of these days.

Granted, the single-engine rate of climb of most twins, even the turbocharged ones, is nothing to write home about. With turbocharging, whatever climb capability is available at sea level is also available at quite considerable altitudes. Without turbocharging, most light twins will be unable to climb at all, once they are a few thousand feet above sea level or when the day is a hot one.

As a general rule, businesses faced with the need to purchase a single-engine or light twin aircraft tend to lean toward one manufacturer or another. They may frequently be influenced by the looks of the airplane, spending less time than they should in analyzing the advantages of one model over another. Conversely, businesses or corporations who are in the market for a cabin-class twin, turboprop or jet are much more prone to do a great deal of exhaustive research, probably because so much more money is at stake. This is unrealistic. A million dollars presents no greater stake for a billion-dollar business. Thus, no matter the actual cost of the aircraft, the time spent in advance in analyzing what is available will minimize the chance of buying the wrong one.

Chapter 5

Time and Cost Comparisons

As a self-employed avaition writer, I am neither a business or a corporation. Much of the traveling which I do in the pursuit of my profession is sufficiently similar to the use of the light aircraft by many businesses.

This chapter will describe an actual trip made in a *Piper Arrow* and, throughout, will compare the times and costs involved with several divergent types of aircraft which might have been used for the same trip (Fig. 5-1). Nothing in this chapter is meant to disparage one particular model or single out another. Not every business trip involves the kind of itinerary shown here. In determining which aircraft is best, the businessman must consider all types of use to which the aircraft is expected to be put.

Flight Plan

The Piper Arrow I flew on this particular trip had a cruising speed, at a reasonably economical power setting, of 130 knots, producing a range of somewhat in excess of 600 nm. I traveled alone which meant that the cost of the trip could not be divided between myself and some passengers. The planned itinerary looked like this: Santa Fe, New Mexico (SAF) to Kerrville (ERV) and then to Mineral Wells, Texas (MWL). From there I flew to Wichita (ICT) and Olathe, Kansas (OJC). Then to New Orleans, Louisiana, (MSY), Mobile, Alabama (MOB), Washington, D.C. (DCA), Reading, Pennsylvania (RDG), Champaign, Illinois (CMI), Cedar Rapids, Iowa (CID), Denver, Colorado (DEN), Hailey, Idaho (SUN) and back to Santa Fe. An initial estimate of the total distance, according to Jeppesen's Low Altitude Flight Planning Chart, added to up to about 5,435 nm or roughly 42 hours of flying.

The most important consideration in planning this flight was to arrange ample time for conferences and discussions at each stop. In this particular trip, the only inflexible dates were the days between May 22 and 25, at least one of which was to be spent at the Reading Air Show. Since it was obvious that I'd have to spend at least one weekend on the road, I tried my best to arrange to spend it in New Orleans, even though that meant that the trip would be cutting into a second weekend. This is the flight and business plan I finally settled on.

May 17, Thursday. Leave Sante Fe at 4:00 a.m. (Mountain Time) for a four-hour 511-nm flight to Kerrville. Arrive Kerrville at 9:00 a.m. (Central Time). Conduct business at the Mooney plant for two hours. Plan to leave about 11:30 for Mineral Wells, a distance of 174 nm. Flight time is 1:20. Arrive in time for a late luncheon meeting with the Edo-Aire Mitchell autopilot people. Arrange for a test flight after lunch to try out one of their newest gimmicks. Leave any time in the late afternoon for Wichita. Distance, 323 nm; time, 2:30. RON (rest over night).

May 18, Friday. Early breakfast meeting at Gates Learjet. Then hop over to Beech Airport for two-hour session there. From there over to Cessna's airport, a quick lunch and a one-hour familiarization flight in the Pressurized Centurion. Takeoff at 3:30 for Olathe's Johnson County Airport. Distance, 164 nm; time, 1:16. Arrange to be met at the airport by someone from King Radio for a late afternoon meeting at the King plant. Try to get back to the airport for a 7:00 p.m. departure. Next destination New Orleans (with refuel and dinner stop at Little Rock, Arkansas). Distance, 632 nm; time 4:50 plus one hour stopover at Little rock. Arrive New Orleans Lakefront Airport at 12:50. Taxi to Royal Orleans Hotel in the French Quarter.

May 19, Saturday. Meetings with the Petroleum Helicopter people, the largest helicopter operators in the world. Then relax and have a good time.

May 20, Sunday. Sleep late, eat well. After dinner, taxi to Lakefront Airport. Leave for Mobile, Alabama. Distance, 113 nm; time, 0:50. RON.

May 21, Monday. Breakfast meeting at Continental Motors. At 11:00 a.m. leave for Washington, D.C. Distance, 782 nm; time, 6:00 hours plus one hour for food and fuel at Greensboro, North Carolina. Arrive Washington National Airport at 7:00 p.m. (Eastern Time). Taxi to hotel.

Fig. 5-1. A 1978 Piper Arrow.

May 22, Tuesday. Meeting at 9:00 a.m. at 800 Independence Avenue with several people at the FAA. Leave Washington National at 12:00 for Reading, Pennsylvania. Distance, 128 nm; time, 1:00. Spend the afternoon at the Reading Air Show.

May 23, Wednesday. Spend the day at the Reading air Show, interviewing various aviation types. In the evening leave for Champaign, Illinois. Distance, 592 nm; time, 4:35. RON.

May 24, Thursday. Morning meeting with Rudy Frasca of Frasca Aviation. At 11:00 a.m. leave Champaign for Cedar Rapids. Distance, 203 nm; time, 1:35. Arrange pickup at the airport by someone from Collins Radio. Luncheon and afternoon meeting at Collins including a demonstration of their new digital weather radar. About 4:00 p.m. leave for Denver. Distance, 607 nm; time, 4:45, plus one hour for fuel and food in North Platte, Nebraska. Arrive Stapleton Field in Denver at 10:45 p.m. (Mountain Time). RON.

May 25, Friday. Breakfast meeting at Jeppesen. Lunch at the airport. Then leave at 1:00 p.m. for Hailey, Idaho. Distance, 537 nm; time, 4:10. Arrive Hailey between 5:00 and 5:30 p.m. Refuel. Then take off again for some aerial photography of Sun Valley at sunset. Land back at Hailey just before total darkness, because the airport is not lighted. Arrange for transportation to Sun Valley Lodge. RON.

May 26, Saturday. Travel around the Sun Valley area by car for article about Sun Valley in summer. After lunch leave for Santa Fe. Distance, 692 nm; time time, 5:20, plus one hour for food and fuel at Grand Junction, Colorado.

67

Santa Fe to Kerrville

Assuming that the weather would have the decency to play along this all looked pretty good. So the next step involved feeding a fair chunk of loot to Ma Bell to firm up all those meetings and appointments.

At 4:00 a.m. on May 17, the thunderstorm of the night before had dissipated, leaving the sky black and studded with stars. The Santa Fe Airport was deserted as was the part-time tower. I taxied to Runway 20 and in the cool of the early morning hour the Arrow climbed better than usual from the 6,344-foot elevation of the airport. I turned southeast toward the sparsely settled expanse of eastern New Mexico and West Texas.

Night flying in this area is not for pilots unfamiliar with the terrain. Towns and roads are few, and with no moon to shed any light, one is on instruments, though technically VFR. By the time I passed Tucumcari the sky began to lighten in the east, revealing some early morning low clouds in the distance ahead. The weather report had forecast clear conditions for the San Antonio area so I decided not to worry. According to the DME (distance measuring equipment) in the airplane, the ground speed was fluctuating between 143 and 152 knots, indicating a fuel-saving tailwind. Since there was little point in arriving at Kerrville ahead of my ETA (estimated time of arrival) I throttled back to about 45 percent, which still moved me along at slightly better than 130 knots, using less than seven gallons an hour.

The clouds below thickened briefly from scattered to broken, and then thinned back to scattered and disappeared. By the time I had passed San Angelo it looked like more clouds ahead, and I asked the San Angelo FSS (flight service station) to check with Kerrville for the current conditions. They came back with a scattered to broken report at about 1,500 feet. I decided to bid my friendly tailwind goodbye and let down to about 3,000 feet, intending to follow the highway from the Junction VOR (very high frequency omni directional radio range) to Kerrville rather than taking a chance on having to fly that fairly unpleasant ADF (automatic direction finder) approach, a non precision approach, using Kerrville's NDB (non-directional beacon). It worked out perfectly (though I could have stayed on top, considering the huge breaks in the overcast at Kerrville). By 8:48 Central Time the airplane was tied down and being refueled.

■ **Piper Arrow:** tach time, 3.8; fuel consumed, 28.5; oil 0; cost, $34.20.

By comparison, let's look at the numbers if any one of four other types of aircraft had been used.

■ **Pressurized Centurion:** tach time, 3.2; fuel consumed, 40.5; oil, 0; cost, $48.60.

■ **Aerostar 601B:** tach time, 2.3; fuel consumed, 55.2; oil, 0; cost, $66.24.

■ **King Air B100:** tach time, 2.1; fuel consumed, 147.3; oil, 0; cost, $162.03.

The accelerate-stop distance for the King Air B100 is 4,000 feet under standard temperature conditions at sea level. Kerrville Airport is at an elevation of 1,616 feet. If the temperature at the time of departure would be expected to be 20 degrees above what is considered standard for that altitude, it might be chancy for that aircraft to attempt takeoff from the 4,400 foot runway, as, under those conditions, the accelerate-stop distance is 5,500 feet. The pilot might therefore decide to land at San Antonio. There would be no appreciable difference in time and fuel, but it would add the cost of a rental car for the drive from San Antonio to Kerrville, plus the time involved in making the drive both ways. In that case the figures would come to the following.

■ **Piper Arrow:** tach time, 2.1; fuel consumed, 147.3; oil, 0; time to drive, 2.0; cost including car rental, $182.03.

■ **CitationI:** tach time, 1.6; fuel consumed, 154.7; oil, 0; cost, $170.17.

Kerrville to Mineral Wells

By the time I was ready to take off for Mineral Wells, the local clouds had disappeared. Once aloft I could see some afternoon thunderstorms starting to build east of my route of flight. This time the wind cut slightly into my ground speed, and it took 1:29 to cover the 174-nm distance.

■ **Piper Arrow:** tach time, 1.5; total 5.3; fuel consumed, 12.9; total 41.4; oil, 0; cost, $15.48; total $49.68.

■ **Pressurized Centurion:** tach time, 1.15; total 4.35; fuel consumed, 14.6; total 55.1; oil, 0; cost, $17.52; total $66.12.

■ **Aerostar 601B:** tach time, 0.8; total 3.1; fuel consumed, 19.2; total 74.4; oil, 0; cost, $23.04; total $89.28.

■ **King Air B100:** tach time, 0.7; total, 2.8; fuel consumed, 49.1; total 196.4; oil, 0; cost, $54.01; total $216.04.

■ **Citation I:** tach time, 0.55 total 2.15; fuel consumed, 53.2; total 207.9; oil, 0; cost, $58.52; total $228.69.

Mineral Wells to Wichita

The 323-nm flight from Mineral Wells to Wichita was at least not boring. The weather report advertised widely scattered thunderstorms all along my route of flight and, except for the widely scattered part, it was right on the nose. The flight service specialist had seemed vaguely upset when I refused to file IFR, but my own preference when jousting with thunderstorm conditions is to be VFR and free to detour hither and yon without having to ask permission. My flight path must have been reminiscent of that of a drunk driver cutting in and out of freeway traffic. Around the various storm cells with their nearly impenetrable rain showers the visibility remained excellent. One such nasty storm, having all but flooded Wichita Municipal, had the good sense to move in time for my somewhat delayed arrival.

■ **Piper Arrow:** tach time, 2.8; total 8.1; fuel consumed, 24.1; total 65.5; oil, 0; cost, $28.92; total $78.60.

■ **Pressurized Centurion:** tach time, 2.1; total 6.45; fuel consumed, 26.6; total 81.7; oil, 0; cost; $31.92; total $98.04.

■ **Aerostar 601B:** tach time, 1.5; total 4.6; fuel consumed, 36.0; total 110.4; oil, 0; cost, $43.20; total $132.48.

■ **King Air B100:** tach time, 1.4; total 4.2; fuel consumed, 98.2; total 294.6; oil, 0; cost, $108.02; total $324.06.

■ **Citation I:** tach time, 1.0; total 3.15; fuel consumed, 96.7; total 304.6; oil, 0; cost, $106.37; total $335.06.

Wichita to Olathe

The activities planned for Wichita turned out to last nearly an hour longer than had planned, but a call to King Radio established that my contact there was willing to meet me later. It was suggested that we hold our meeting over dinner. The late afternoon was fairly hot and humid for May with thunderstorms blossoming as usual. Except for some uncomfortable turbulence, the 164-nm flight to Olathe's Johnson County Airport as uneventful.

■ **Piper Arrow:** tach time, 1.3; total 9.4; fuel consumed, 10.4; total 75.9, oil: 0; cost, $12.48; total $91.08.

■ **Pressurized Centurion:** tach time, 1.06; total 7.51; fuel consumed, 13.25; total 94.95; oil, 0; cost, $15.90; total $113.94.

■ **Aerostar 601B:** tach time 0.75; total 5.35; fuel consumed, 18.0; ttoal 128.4; oil, 0; cost, $21.60; total $154.08.

■ **King Air B100:** tach time, 0.68; total 4.88; fuel consumed 47.7; total 342.3; oil, 0; cost, $52.47; total $376.53.

■ **Citation I:** tach time, 0.51; total 3.66; fuel consumed, 49.3; total 353.9; oil, 0; cost, $54.28; total $389.29.

Olathe to New Orleans

The next leg was the third longest of the entire trip, 632 nm, and beyond the safe range of the airplane and, for that matter, the pilot. After a full day of meetings, I was beginning to feel a bit weary. I finally got off the ground at 9:15 p.m., which meant flying through the better part of the night if I insisted on getting all the way to New Orleans. I decided to keep an open mind and headed south. The perpetual thunderstorms had relaxed somewhat and moon and stars peeked through the ever widening breaks in the towering overcast. I hooked the autopilot to the appropriate VORs and tried, without much success, to tune in a talk show on the ADF to help keep me awake. I have never been able to figure out why it appears to be so difficult to produce an ADF that, on the broadcast band, sounds close to as good as the cheapest car radio. I wished I had thought of asking the people at King, but I hadn't.

Past Fayetteville the weather took a hand in making me forget my increasing sleepiness. The sky disappeared and was replaced by a black mess that the local FSS described as "4,000 overcast with light drizzle." I briefly considered air-filing IFR, but the visibility below the clouds remained pretty good despite the drizzle. I went down to 4,000 feet msl which would keep me a little over 1,000 feet above the mountains that lie between Fayetteville and Little Rock. I switched the Number One to Fort Smith and, getting a 63-degrees-FROM reading, I knew that most of the mountains were behind me.

The radar advisory people at Little Rock, apparently having nothing much else to do at this hour of the night, insisted on telling me how to get to the airport even after I had the runway in sight. At least this time their vectors didn't involve any undue detours. It was close to midnight by the time the airplane was tied down, and I decided the hell with New Orleans. Arkansas would be as good a place to spend the night as any.

■ **Piper Arrow:** tach time, 2.6; total 12.0; fuel consumed, 21.1; total 97.0; oil, 1 quart; cost, $26.82; total $117.90.

Because of the faster cruising speed and greater range of the other aircraft, and the greater altitudes at which they would have made the trip to New Orleans non-stop.

The next morning, with the early sun lighting a cloudless sky, I was airborne by 7:15 a.m. for the remaining 303 nm to New

Orleans. Two hours later the vast expanse of Lake Pontchartrain lay dead ahead with New Orleans' Lakefront Airport at the far shore.

■ **Piper Arrow:** tach time, 2.3; total 14.3; fuel consumed, 18.1; total 115.1; oil, 0; total 1; cost, $21.72; total $139.62.

■ **Pressurized Centurion:** tach time, 4.08; total 11.59 fuel consumed, 51.7; total 146.65; oil, 1 quart; cost, $62.04; total $175.98.

■ **Aerostar 601B:** tach time, 2.9; total 8.28; fuel consumed, 69.6; total 198.0; oil cost; $83.52; total $237.60.

■ **King Air B100:** tach time, 2.62; total 7.5; fuel consumed, 183.8; total 526.1; oil, 0; cost, $202.18; total $578.71.

■ **Citation I:** tach time, 1.97; total 5.63; fuel consumed, 190.5; total 544.4; oil; 0; cost, $209.55; total $598.84.

New Orleans to Mobile

After some hours of work and a day and a half of a fun time in New Orleans, topped off by one of those incomparable dinners that the city is famous for, I left Sunday evening for Mobile. It was a short and uneventful 113-nm hop.

■ **Piper Arrow:** tach time, 0.8; total 15.1; fuel consumed, 6.4; total 121.5; oil, 0; total 1; cost $7.68; total $147.30.

■ **Pressurized Centurion:** tach time, 0.73; total 12.32; fuel consumed, 9.25; total 155.9; oil, 0; total 1; cost, $11.10; total $187.08.

■ **Aerostar 601B:** tach time, 0.52; total 8.8; fuel consumed, 12.5; total 210.5; oil, 0; cost, $15.00; total $252.60.

■ **King Air B100:** tach time, 0.47; total 7.97; fuel consumed, 16.9; total 543.0; oil, 0; cost, $18.59; total $597.30.

■ **Citation I:** tach time, 0.35; total 5.98; fuel consumed, 33.85; total 578.25; oil, 0; cost; $39.44; total $638.28.

Mobile to Washington

The next leg was the longest of the trip, 782 nm, to Washington D.C., with a fuel stop planned for Greensboro, North Carolina. I had hoped to leave before lunch, but as it turned out we had lunch in Mobile and it was close to 2:00 p.m. before I was airborne. The weather report indicated a healthy tailwind at 9,000 and a better one at 12,000. I initially climbed to 9,500 where the DME reported a ground speed of close to 152 knots. A variety of clouds and rain showers was forecast for my route, with Washington expecting a broken overcast with good visibilities for my ETA. But Greensboro didn't sound too promising, and I decided that I'd refuel whereever I'd find decent weather conditions en route.

I hadn't been flying an hour when the tops of the undercast pushed me up another 2,000 feet to 11,500, increasing my ground speed by six or seven knots. Having nothing else to do while the autopilot flew the airplane, I studied the charts and decided that it would be safe to refuel anywhere past a point some 100 nm northeast of Atlanta in order to make the balance of the flight non-stop. I also figured out that at my current ground speed and rate of fuel flow I could actually make Washington non-stop. I quickly discarded that idea, knowing full well that nothing can be more foolish than to bet one's life on a continued tailwind.

Atlanta came and passed some two miles beneath, hidden by solid clouds. I started to let my eyes roam for dark colored areas ahead that might indicate a break through which a descent for a fuel stop would be easy. As must be obvious by now, I don't particularly enjoy flying IFR. I feel comfortable in the knowledge that I can if I have to, but to me there is something obnoxious about having people on the ground tell me what to do. This doesn't mean that I think everyone should do as I do, not at all. It is simply that I personally enjoy flying VFR whenever possible.

When the cloud tops are full of bumps and valleys there are nearly always chasms through which the ground becomes visible, if only for moments at a time. And that day was no exception. With the OBI (omni-bearing indicator) locked firmly to the Spartanburg VOR, I found a huge canyon in the clouds. Advised by the FSS that the local weather indicated a 3,000-foot ceiling with breaks in the overcast and five-mile visibility, I throttled back to below gear speed and put the gear down. For the next seven or eight minutes I circled down at 1,000 fpm (feet per minute) safely clear of clouds, until I was below the whole mess.

With all tanks again filled to the brim and some coffee and doughnuts inside myself, I filed IFR to VFR on top. I was loath to abandon those beautiful tailwinds up there. Clear at 9,000, I cancelled IFR and continued up to 11,500, again scooting along at better than 150 knots toward Washington.

An hour had been lost somewhere along the way when crossing from Central to Eastern Time. It was nearly 9:00 p.m. by the time I identified myself to the Washington TCA (terminal control area) people, realizing that I had forgotten to make a reservation. But, with the high-density traffic hours past, they didn't seem to care one way or other other. The weather in the Washington area had turned from broken to scattered, and the approach to Washington National was a piece of cake.

■ **Pieper Arrow:** tach time; 5.2; total 20.3; fuel consumed, 38.1; total 159.6; 0; total 1; cost, $45.72; total $193.02.

■ **Pressurized Centurion:** tach time, 5.0; total 17.32; fuel consumed, 63.3; total 219.2; oil, 0; total 1; cost, $75.96; total $263.04.

■ **Aerostar 601B:** tach time, 3.55; total 12.3; fuel consumed, 85.2; total 295.7; oil, 2 quarts; cost, $105.24; total $357.84.

■ **King Air B100:** tach time, 3.24; total 11.21; fuel consumed, 116.5; total 659.5; oil, 2 quarts; cost, $128.15; total $725.45.

■ **Citation I:** tach time, 2.4; total 8.38; fuel consumed, 232.1; total 810.35; oil, 0; cost, $255.31; total $893.59.

Washington to Reading

The next day was hot and humid; visibility was reported an optimistic three miles in haze. With Reading only 128 nm away, I stayed low. After passing the Lancaster VOR, I contacted the Reading tower to be funneled into the steady stream of traffic arriving for the air show. Anyone who has never experienced the kind of aerial madness that takes place anually at Reading (and Oshkosh, the Reno Air Races, etc.) will find it hard to understand how all these airplanes manage to stay clear of one another, as they converge in a steady stream on the approach end of the active runway. But it works, and much credit must go to the harassed tower controllers who somehow manage to maintain order and, in turn, safety for all.

■ **Piper Arrow:** tach time (including a 20-minute hold while waiting for clearance to land) 1.3; total 21.6; fuel consumed, 10.2; total 169.8; oil 0; total 1; cost, $12.24; total $205.26.

■ **Pressurized Centurion:** tach time (including 20-minute hold), 1.15; total 18.47; fuel consumed, 14.57; total 233.77; oil, 0; total 1; cost, $17.48; total $280.52.

■ **Aerostar 601B:** tach time (including only five-minute hold because he filed IFR), 0.7; total 13.0; fuel consumed, 16.8; total 312.5; oil, 0; total 2; cost, $15.60; total $373.44.

■ **King Air B100:** tach time (including five-minute hold) 0.6; total 11.81; fuel consumed, 42.09; total 701.59; oil 0; total 2; cost, $46.30; total $771.75.

■ **Citation I:** tach time (including five-minute hold), 0.49; total 8.87; fuel consumed, 47.4; total 857.75; oil, 0; cost, $52.14; total $945.73.

Reading to Champaign

Reading is Reading. Suffice it to say that despite the somewhat shaky economy of the country as a whole, the aviation business continued to boom. Considering the 2,817 nm which I had just flown at a total cost of $205.26, I was ample proof of why. I stayed until the following evening and then started off on the 592 nm flight to Champiagn, Illinios, expecting to stop somewhere en route for fuel and RON. This expectation became an unavoidable reality as headwinds reduced my ground speed to below 120 knots. I remembered the Sheraton Inn on the Columbus Airport; that seemed as good a place as any. The weather called for 3,000 to 5,000-foot overcast all along the way, keeping me at about 1,500 feet agl (above ground level), resulting in a considerable increase in fuel flow.

The next morning I started early from Columbus on a beautifully clear morning. I arrived in Champaign, after gaining an hour by crossing into the Central Time zone, in time for a late breakfast.

■ **Piper Arrow:** tach time, 4.9 total 26.5; fuel consumed, 43.9; total 213.7; oil, 1, total 2; cost, $52.68; total $257.94.

■ **Pressurized Centurion:** tach time, 3.9; total 22.37; fuel consumed, 49.4; total 283.17; oil, 1; total 2; cost, $60.78; total $341.30.

■ **Aerostar 601B:** tach time, 2.78; total 15.78; fuel consumed, 66.72; total 379.22; oil, 0; total 2; cost, $80.06; total $453.50.

■ **King Air B100:** tach time, 2.5; total 14.31; fuel consumed; 175.3; total 876.89; oil, 0; total 2; cost, $192.83; total $964.58.

■ **Citation I:** tach time, 1.88; total 10,75; fuel consumed, $199.98; total $1,145.71.

Champaign to Cedar Rapids

By 11:30 I was back in the airplane. Shortly after 1:00 p.m. I landed at Cedar Rapids, Iowa, some 203 nm farther northwest.

■ **Piper Arrow:** tach time, 1.6; total 28.1; fuel consumed, 14.1; total 227.8; oil 0; total 2; cost, $16.92; total $274.86.

■ **Pressurized Centurion:** tach time, 1.31; total 23.68; fuel consumed, 16.59; total 299.76; oil 0; total 2; cost, $19.91; total $361.21.

■ **Aerostar 601B:** tach time, 0.93; total 16.71; fuel consumed, 22.32; total 401.54; oil, 0; total 2; cost, $26.78; total $480.28.

■ **King Air B100:** tach time, 0.84; total 15.15; fuel consumed, 83.51; total 960.4; oil, 0; total 2; cost, $91.86; total $1,056.44.

■ **Citation I:** tach time, 0.63; total 11.38; fuel consumed, 60.93; total 1,100.48; oil, 0; total 2; cost, $67.02; total $1,212.73.

Cedar Rapids to Denver

Somehow I always feel better once I get west of the Mississippi. Its as if one could smell the Rockies with their crystal-clear air and 100-mile-plus visibilities. Therefore, even though it had been a long day already, I felt a touch of exhileration as I took off in mid-afternoon from Cedar Rapids toward North Platte and Denver, the forecast widely scattered thunderstorms not withstanding. With the winds at 9,000 said to be less than 10 knots in the wrong direction, I climbed to 8,500, figuring that the reduced fuel flow at altitude was worth the slight reduction in ground speed. The thunderstorms presented no major problem. By the time the last daylight disappeared below the western horizon, I was passing Grand Island with a good two-thirds of my fuel still in the tanks. This meant that I should be able to get to Denver non-stop easily, especially since the winds in that area tend to die down after dark. I continued to sit up there fat and happy, thinking that the vague dark outline ahead might just be the silhouette of the eastern edge of the Rockies.

But the illusion didn't last long. The dark shape continued to grow in height and it was soon obvious that what I was heading for was a bunch of towering cumulus, probably three times the height of the highest Rocky peaks. A call to the Hayes Center FSS produced information of a thunderstorm over the Akron-Washington Airport, with Denver reporting clear and towering cumulus east. I asked about Sidney, some 55 nm north of Akron, and received a report of clear with towering cumulus south. A check on Thurman, 26 nm south of Akron, produced information of a thunderstorm overhead and heavy rain showers all quadrants. Obviously I would have to detour to the north, possibly as far as Sidney, adding some 20 or 30 nm to the 170-nm straight line distance. A check of the fuel showed about 22 usable gallons remaining, sufficient for nearly three hours at the current economy-cruise setting. I would be able to get to Denver, no matter how much of a detour I'd have to fly. So I twisted the autopilot slightly to the right, heading for what I assumed to be a spot about halfway between Akron and Sidney.

The clouds grew taller and more ominous. The air began to get bumpy. With the terrain beneath at about 5,000 feet, I got down to 6,000 to see how far north the core of that storm extended. A lightish glow indicative of night sky, plus occasional lights on the ground at a considerable distance, seemed to indicate clear sailing slightly to the right of my current heading. Straight ahead and to the left everything was pitch black, punctuated by intermittent but spectacular lightning.

To make a long and bumpy story short, the detour stretched much farther than I had anticipated. I landed eventually at Denver's Stapleton Field with a slightly disconcerting 3.5 usable gallons left in the tanks. It would have been better if I had stopped to refuel in either North Platte or Grand Island, as originally planned.

■ **Piper Arrow**: tach time, 5.9; total 34.0; fuel consumed; 44.5; total 272.3; oil 1; total 3; cost $53.40; total $328.26.

■ **Pressurized Centurion**: tach time, 4.0; total 27.68; fuel consumed, 50.67; total 350.43; oil, 0; total 2; cost, $60.80; total $422.01.

■ **Aerostar 601B**:tach time, 2.82; total 18.99; fuel consumed, 67.68; total 469.22; oil, 0; total 2; cost, $81.22; total $561.50.

■ King Air B100: tach time, 2.52; total 17.67; fuel consumed, 176.78; total 1,137.18; oil, 0; total 2; cost, $194.46; total $1,250.90.

■ **Citation I**: tach time, 1.9; total 12.28; fuel consumed, 183.76; total 1,284.24; oil, 0; total 2; cost, $202.14; total $1,414.87.

Denver to Hailey

The flight the next day was one I was looking forward to because it would take me over some of the most spectacular country anywhere. Based on the weather forecast (visibilities between 60 and 100 miles) and winds at 12,000 and 15,000 (280 degrees at 10 to 15 knots), the time en route would be just under 4.5 hours. Since Hailey's Friedman Memorial Airport is not lighted, I figured I'd better be off the ground not later than 1:00 p.m.

Well, as usual, things dragged out a bit. I was airborne by 1:45, climbing at somewhere between the best rate and the best angle of climb to get close to the 14,000 feet that is the necessary minimum for a west-northwest departure from Denver. The route I was taking, direct from Denver to Rock Springs, Pocatello, and Hailey, is off any Victor airways. It is marked on the Jeppesens in green as J-20. Except for Rock Springs and Pocatello, there are no VORs along the route. With the direct distance from Denver to Rock Springs being 217nm, and the one from there to Pocatello over 170 nm, the usual type of navigation from VOR to VOR is impossible. But there are VORs at reasonable reception distances to either side of my proposed route. Having recently installed a Foster Airdata 511 RNAV (area navigation) system, I would now have a chance to see how it worked out in practice.

Once having leveled off at somewhat above 14,000 feet to clear those still snow-covered rocks north of Kremling, I used the Laramie VOR. I moved it electronically some 50 nm along its 210-degree radial which put it right on my nose. It worked perfectly except for brief moments when the mountains interfered with reception. All along the DME confirmed a ground speed of slightly better than 120 knots, meaning that I could expect to arrive at Hailey around 6:00 p.m. with ample daylight to spare.

■ **Piper Arrow**: tach time, 4.4; total 38.4; fuel consumed, 33.0 total 305.3; oil, 0; total 3; cost, $39.60; total $367.86.

■ **Pressurized Centurion**: tach time, 3.53; total 31.21; fuel consumed, 44.71; total 395.14; oil, 1; total 3; cost, $55.15; total $477.16

■ **Aerostar 601B**: tach time, 2.49; total 21.48; fuel consumed, 59.76; total 528.98; oil, 2; total 4; cost, $74.71; total $636.21.

■ **King Air B100**: tach time, 2.23; total 19.9; fuel consumed; 156.43; total 1,293.61; oil, 2; total 4; cost, $175.07; total 1,425.97.

■ **Citation I**. tach time, 1.68; total 13.96; fuel consumed, 162.48; total 1,446.72; oil, 0; total 2; cost, $178.73; total $1,593.60.

Home to Santa Fe

The next day, Saturday, involved the 692-nm flight home to Santa Fe, again overflying breathtaking scenery just far enough for a fuel stop, probably in Grand Junction, unless a healthy tailwind would make a stop unnecessary. By the time the work in the Sun Valley area was finished it was going on 3:00 p.m. It was nearly 3:45 by the time I was airborne, heading southeastward toward Salt Lake City. The hoped for tailwind did materialize bringing with it the kind of turbulence that is par for the course for the Rockies on spring and summer afternoons. When you live in a place like Santa Fe you get used to that sort of thing and learn to simply relax every muscle in your body, letting the airplane rise and fall with the up and downdrafts. You know that there is no point in trying to fight it. The DME indicated a healthy 150 knots ground speed while the typical afternoon cloud buildups started to develop over the higher mountain tops. But while they are a daily occurrence during spring and summer in the Rockies, they rarely merge into those impenetrable squall lines. I felt reasonably certain that I'd be able to get home without the need for extended detours. This time I did have a Victor airway, V-484, to follow at least as far as Montrose, after which I planned to fly direct across the spectacular San Juan mountain range to Santa Fe.

With the turbulence becoming increasingly unpleasant, I throttled back to a lower airspeed. Still the ground speed hovered around 150 knots, apparently as the result of an increase in the tailwind. The portable oxygen system came in handy as occasional sustained updrafts would push the airplane up to above 16,000 feet. As I locked onto the Grand Junction VOR it was obvious that I was far ahead of my ETA. I decided to go on to Santa Fe non-stop. South of Grand Junction the cumulus buildups increased with occasional lightning in the bigger ones. There was ample room between the clouds to continue on a more or less straight line. By the time I finally landed at Santa Fe, I still had nearly 12 gallons of usable fuel in the tanks.

■ **Piper Arrow**: tach time, 4.9; total 43.3; fuel consumed, 36.3; total 341.6; oil 1; total 4; cost, $43.56; total $411.42.

■ **Pressurized Centurion**: tach time, 4.3; total 35.51; fuel consumed; 54.47; total 449.61; oil, 0; total 3; cost, $65.36; total $542.52.

■ **Aerostar 601B** tach time, 3.07; total 24.55 fuel consumed, 73.68; total 602.66; oil 0; total 4; cost, $88.42; total $724.63.

■ **King Air B100**: tach time, 2.78; total 22.68; fuel consumed, 195; total 1,488.61; oil 0; total 4; cost, $214.50; total $1,640.47.

■ **Citation I**: tach time, 2.06; total 16.02; fuel consumed, 199.23; total 1,645.95; oil, 0; total 2; cost, $ 219.15; total $1,812,75.

Trip Summary

In all the above computations the avgas is figured at $1.20 per gallon, the jet fuel at $1.10 per gallon, and oil at $1.50 per quart. Not included are reserves for major overhaul, insurance, etc., and such miscellaneous items as tiedown fees, landing fees and such. These items would add approximately $14.22 per hour, or a total of $615.73 to the cost of the trip for the Arrow. In the cases of the other airplanes, these expenses amount to Pressurized Centurion: $17.80 per hour $632.08 total; Aerostar 601B: $33.52 per hour $822.92 total; King Air B100: $129.34 per hour $2,933.43 total; Citation I: $193.94 per hour, $3,106.92 total.

In summary the entire trip looked like this: total number of days, 10; number of cities in which business was conducted, 12; nautical miles flown, 5,448; number of hours spent in business meetings and activities, 57. In this particular case it is doubtful that using the faster aircraft would have saved a meaningful amount of time, primarily because in the Arrow much of the flying took place at night. Granted, the Citation spent a total of 26:10 hours less in the air than did the Arrow. By carefully arranging the appointments and sticking to the predetermined schedule, it might have gotten home a day earlier. But since the day saved would have been a Saturday, this would not have warranted the extra cost.

What can be learned from this is that the faster the airplane, the better it does over long distances. A large number of relatively short hops can just as easily and more cheaply be accomplished in a slower aircraft.

Chapter 6
Dollars and Cents

What does it actually cost to operate an airplane, any kind of an airplane? Few of us ever bother to figure it out in detail. Why? The reason might be because we airplane owners and operators prefer to kid ourselves and others about the actual cost, or maybe because it requires a fair amount of complicated arithmetic.

On the surface it all looks very simple. There is the actual cost of the airplane itself, and then there is the expense of feeding it with fuel and oil. What else? Well, there is insurance, and the charge for tiedown or hangar space. Oh, well, then there are those periodic inspections. Eventually there will be a major overhaul. But that's still a long way off. Let's break all this down and see what we come up with.

Cost of Purchase

The first thing that often tends to be a bit shocking is the difference between the so-called manufacturer's suggested retail price of the airplane itself, and the actual cost when we add the kind of avionics we want—autopilot, de-icing systems and various other options. Some manufacturers deliver their airplanes with at least some of this equipment included in the base price. Others simply put a price tag on the "green" airplane, meaning one that can just barely be legally flown with its standard equipment. Thus, there is no way to establish a hard and fast rule for the relationship between the base price and the equipped price. Cessna, for instance, sells most of its piston-engine aircraft in two or three versions, the difference being the standard equipment included in the price. Thus, a *Cessna 310*, as an example, comes in two versions, the basic 310 and the 310 II. The price of the basic 310, as of 1979, is $133,490 and that of the 310 II $158,990, a difference of $25,500.

Now let's look at the difference between the two airplanes. Among the flight instruments, the only difference is the outside-air temperature indicator, which is optional on the 310 and standard on the 310 II. Among the engine instruments it's an EGT (exhaust gas temperature gauge), which is standard on the II and optional on the 310. Strangely enough, in the area of controls, dual controls are optional on the 310, standard on th II (though I can't remember having ever seen a Cessna airplane without dual controls). In terms of the so-called flight-deck instruments, electric elevator trim is standard on the II only. Now to lighting. A second landing light in the right tip tank, a rotating beacon and a taxi light are optional in the basic airplane and standard in the II. Also optional in one and standard in the other are auxiliary fuel tanks, six-place seating, static dischargers, nosewheel fenders (whatever they are), ground-service plug receptacle, basic avionics kit, autopilot and transponder.

The total cost for all of these goodies, when ordered separately, comes to $27,440. In other words, if we like the type of avionics which Cessna puts into its II airplanes, then we actually save $1,940 by buying the II. But there is more. If we want air conditioning, it's $7,765. A complete de-icing system for flight into known icing conditions comes to $8,300, plus $1,450 for a different type of alternator which is needed for it. And there are bound to be some additions to the avionics. A reasonably priced DME will add, say, $3,000. An encoding altimeter adds another $1,000 And RNAV, which is becoming increasingly important, will cost another $3,000. Weather radar starts at around $7,000 and goes up from there. Thus, in order to have a reasonably well-equipped all-weather IFR airplane, we have now spent $190,505, which is $57,015 more than the cost of the basic 310.

Financing the Purchase

Once we've gotten over that shock, we now go to our friendly lending institution and arrange to finance our close to $200,000 baby with a six-year installment agreement. With luck we'll have to plunk down $40,000 in cash (or a trade-in), and then have to pay monthly installments of roughly $3,200 for the next 72 months. (If interest rates keep going the way they have been recently, it may be more than that.) And then there is the sales tax. Assuming we're lucky enough to be buying in a state with a 4.25 percent sales tax, such as New Mexico, the tax alone comes to $8,096.46. (In a state with seven percent sales tax, this would add up to $13,335.35).

Fig. 6-1. The brand new bird is now sitting at the airport.

Adding to this some registration fees or whatever silly extras always seem to creep in, the initial cash outlay is going to be somewhere between $50,000 and $55,000.

Insurance and Maintenance Expenses

Okay, we've signed on the dotted line and have written a check for our $50,000 plus. The brand new shiny bird is now sitting at the airport (Fig. 6-1). Depending on the city in which we live and the airport at which we decide to keep the airplane, tiedown space will cost us anywhere from $40 to $100 a month. If we live in a part of the country where weather is a factor, we may want to keep it in a hangar, in which case the monthly charge will be between $100 and $200. Let's take $100 as a happy medium. We've added $1,200 to the annual fixed cost. But we're certainly not going to fly without adequate liability insurance coverage. The friendly lender will insist that we insure the hull of the aircraft (meaning the aircraft with everything in it) against all conceivable risk. The entire insurance package is likely to run somewhere close to five percent of the cost of the airplane per year, or, in this case $9,225.25.

Then there is routine maintenance and the required annual inspection, plus all manner of miscellaneous expense, amounting to, and this is strictly an educated guess, $3,000. So, for the pleasure of owning an airplane, without having so far flown a single mile, we are committed to an annual outlay of $101,825.25 for the first year, and $51,825.25 for the succeeding six years. Assuming that we will be using the airplane 500 hours each year, the fixed costs per hour will come to $203.65. per hour for the first year and $103.65 per hour for the succeeding six years. Assuming that our average cruising speed is 180 knots, that becomes $1.13 per nautical mile during the first year and $0.58 from then on.

While these figures may seem way too high to be able to be jsutified under average travel conditions, it must be remembered that at the end of those six years we own an airplane free and clear. We can probably sell it for about 60 or 70 percent of what we paid for it (more if inflation keeps going as it is). When rid of the monthly installment payments, we can probably cut our insurance costs in half. At that point, the hourly portion of the fixed costs will then be reduced to $17.63 which figures out as 10 cents per nautical miles.

Flying Expenses

So much for the fixed costs. Now we have to look at what we have to spend in order to actually fly the airplane. First there is fuel. At a reasonable power setting the 310 burns 164 pounds per hour. At 500 hours of utilization a year that comes to 82,000 pounds or 13,667 gallons which, at $1.20 per gallon, comes to $16,400. Oil doesn't come to much. Assuming we use two quarts every 10 hours, it comes to $150 a year, at $1.50 per quart. Miscellaneous landing fees, away-from-home tiedowns, en-route repairs and the like will probably amount to not less than $2,000 a year with 500-hour utilization.

Then there is that distant future bugaboo, the major overhaul. For the type of engine which powers the 310, this is likely to cost about $12,000 per engine or a total of $24,000 when the time comes. And the time does come every 1,500 hours, in other words, once every three years. Reserves for the overhaul amount to $16 per hour or, for a 500-hour year, to $8,000. The totals in terms of variables costs for a typical 500-hour year then come to $26,550. That's $53.10 per hour to be added to the fixed costs of $203.65 the first year, $103.65 for years two through six, and $17.63 starting with the seventh year. This brings the totals to $256.75, $156.75 and $70.73, and per mile costs to $1.43, 87 cents and 39 cents. This still looks expensive. Considering the saving of valuable time, the added business opportunities and other intangible benefits, it isn't really so bad. Whoever said flying was cheap?

Cost Figures for Other Models

So far we have used the Cessna 310 as an example. Now, without repeating all the gory details, let's take a quick look at what these figures would come to in a few other models. We have picked one in each category, selecting those which are representative and among the most popular.

Fig. 6-2. The most popular aircraft ever built is the Cessna Skyhawk.

■ **Fixed-Gear Singles:** *Cessna Skyhawk.*
See Fig. 6-2.
Base price: $33,150
Adequately equipped price: $40,000
Down payment: $8,000
Sales tax (5 percent): $2,000
Monthly payments (72 months): $666.67
Insurance per year: $2,000
Tiedown/hangar & miscellaneous fixed costs (year):
$1,200
Fuel for 500 hours (gallons): 3,500
Fuel for 500 hours (cost at $1.20 per gal.): $4,200
Oil (1 quart per 10 hours at $1.50): $75.00
Reserve for overhaul (per hour): $2.50
Miscellaneous variable costs (per year): $1,000.00
Cost per hour (yr. 1/yr. 2-6/yr. 7+): $55.45/$35.45/
$17.45
Cost per nm (yr. 1/yr. 2-6/yr. 7+): $0.48/$0.31/$0.15
■ **Retractable-Gear Singles:** *Beech Bonanza V35.*
See Fig. 6-3.
Base price: $89,284
Adequately equipped price: $115,000
Down payment: $23,000
Sales tax (5 percent): $5,750
Monthly payments (72 months): $1,916.67
Insurance per year: $5,750
Tiedown/hangar & miscellaneous fixed costs (year):
$1,200
Fuel for 500 hours (gallons): 5,750
Fuel for 500 hours (cost at $1.20 per gallon): $6,900

85

Fig. 6-3. The favorite aircraft of the professional man, the Beech Bonanza.

Oil (1 quart per 10 hours at $1.50): $75
Reserve for overhaul (per hour): $4.67
Miscellaneous variable costs (per year): $1,000
Cost per hour (yr. 1/yr. 2-6/yr.7+): $138.02/$80.52/
$28.77
Cost per nm (yr. 1/yr. 2-6/yr. 7+): $0.86/$0.50/$0.18

■ **Owner Flown Twins:** *Cessna 310* **Cabin-Class Twins:** *Piper Navajo* $208.540
Adequately equipped price: $300,000
Down payment: $60,000
Sales tax (5 percent): $15,000
Monthly payments (72 months): $5,000
Tiedown/hangar & miscellaneous fixed costs per (year):
$2,000
Fuel for 500 hours (gallons): 72,000
Fuel for 500 hours (cost at $1.20 per gallon): $86,400
Oil (2 quarts per 10 hours at $1.50): $150
Reserve for overhaul (per hour): $11.11
Miscellaneous variable costs (per year): $1,800
Cost per hour (yr. 1/yr. 2-6/yr. 7+): $491.81/ See Fig.
6-4. $341.81/$206.81
Cost per nm (yr. 1/yr. 2-6/yr. 7+): $2.35/$1.64/$0.99

■ **Turboprops:** *Piper Cheyenne II*
See Fig. 6-5.
Base price: $635,890
Adequately equipped price: $835,000
Down payment: $167,000
Sales tax (5 percent): $41,750
Monthly payments (72 months): $13,916.67
Insurance per year: $41,750

Fig. 6-4. The cabin-class Piper Navajo.

Tiedown/hangar & miscellaneous fixed costs (year): $3,000

Professional pilot (salary & miscellaneous, year): $25,000

Fuel for 500 hours (gallons): 41,045

Fuel for 500 hours (cost at $1.10 per gallon): $45,149.50

Oil (4 quarts per 10 hours at $1.50): $300

Reserve for overhaul (per hour): $16

Miscellaneous variable costs (per year): $2,500

Cost per hour (yr. 1/yr. 2-6/yr.7+): $1,002.90/ $585.40/$209.65

Cost per nm (yr. 1/yr. 2-6/yr. 7+): $3.54/$2.07/$0.74

■ **Light Jet:** *Gates Learjet 24*

See Fig. 6-6.

Base price: $1,585,000

Adequately equipped price: $1,650,000

Down payment: $330,000

Fig. 6-5. The turboprop outgrowth of the Navajo, the Piper Cheyenne.

Fig. 6-6. Gates Learjet 24.

Sales tax (5 percent): $82,500
Monthly payments (72 months): $27,500
Insurance per year: $82,500
Tiedown/hangar & miscellaeous fixed costs (year): $5,000
Professional pilots (2) (salary & miscellaneous, year): $45,000
Fuel for 500 hours (gallons): 89,552
Fuel for 500 hours (cost at $1.10 per gallon): $98,507.46
Oil (4 quarts per 10 hours at $1.50): $300
Reserve for overhaul (per hour): $21.67
Miscellaneous variable costs (per year): $3,500
Cost per hour (yr. 1/yr. 2-6/yr. 7+): $1,976.28/$1,151.28/$408.78
Cost per nm (yr. 1/yr. 2-6/yr. 7+): $4.39/$2.56/$0.91
■ **Heavy Jet:** *Dassault Falcon 20*
Base price: $4,450,000
Adequately equipped price: $5,000,000
Down payment: $1,000,000
Sales tax (5 percent): $250,000
Monthly payments (72 months): $83,333,33
Insurance per year: $250,000
Tiedown/hangar & miscellaneous fixed costs (year): $5,000

Professional pilots (2) (salary & miscellaneous, year): $45,000

Fuel for 500 hours (gallons): 126,866

Fuel for 500 hours (cost at $1.10 per gallon): $139,552.23

Oil (4 quarts per 10 hours at $1.50): $300

Reserve for overhaul (per hour): $23.33

Miscellaneous variable costs (per year): $3,500

Cost per hour (yr. 1/yr. 2-6/yr. 7+): $5,401.03/$2,910.03/$660.03

Cost per nm (yr. 1/yr. 2-6/yr. 7+): $12.02/$6.47/$1.47

Chapter 7
Taxes And Insurance

Taxes and insurance are subjects most of us prefer not to think about. We hire others to do that thinking and then reluctantly pay whatever it is they tell us we have to. Realizing that government is a necessary evil, we use its services and generally are willing to pay a reasonable price for these services. Still, there is no point in paying more than we have to. If the lawmakers provide loopholes that make the tax laws look like a piece of Swiss cheese, it is our inalienable right to take advantage of all that are available to us. As aircraft owners we face some special tax problems, and in the following pages we'll try and analyze these problems in a general way.

Dealing with the IRS

Many of us have developed a mental block about taxes and tax laws and have therefore decided that it is preferable to pay an accountant to deal with the everchanging convolutions of the rules. The trouble is that most accountants (and most Internal Revenue Service (IRS) men) know little if anything about aviation. If we use an airplane in our business or profession and, therefore, our annual aviation-related expenses are considerable, it might be worthwhile to seek out an accountant who specializes in aviation matters and let him handle that portion of our taxes.

The owner (lessee, renter) of an aircraft, be it and individual or a company, may deduct all flying costs connected with the performance, promotion or furtherance of business. To do this he should be prepared to be able to prove to the IRS that the sometimes greater cost of operating an aircraft in relation to airline fares or automotive expense is justified. It results in increased business, greater effectiveness and productivity than would be available with other modes of transportation.

If the aircraft is exclusively used for business, this is a relatively simple matter. All expenses related to ownership and operation are simply thrown into the business deductions hopper. Where it gets complicated is in cases where the aircraft is used for business part of the time, but at other times serves as a personal vehicle transporting family or friends on vacations and such. In such instances it is important to have clear records of the hours flown for business and those used in non-business flying. Based on the percentage of total hours which each type of activity represents, the fixed costs should then be divided accordingly. Only the percentage of the fixed costs which coincides with the percentage of business travel can be declared as a deduction.

Quite often, especially in cases where an individual uses an airplane in the conduct of his profession, the fact that aircraft costs show up on the Schedule C tends to draw attention to the return. Ownership of an aircraft is still fairly unusual and, to the uninformed, excessively expensive. This can be an added incentive for the IRS to start an audit, simply because the particular individual in the IRS hasn't got the faintest idea about the realities associated with aviation. It is then particularly important that no attempt has been made to include non-business use as a deductible item.

Investment Tax Credit

Investment tax credit is one of those gimmicks the government has invented as a tool to manipulate the economy. Whenever the economy is in bad shape, the investment tax credit allowance is likely to be raised, as this will encourage companies to make large capital investments which, in turn, tend to reduce unemployment. To the potential aircraft operator the tax credit means that if he buys a new aircraft and intends to keep it for a certain minimum period of time, he is entitled to deduct a portion of the cost of the aircraft during the first year of ownership. The specific rules governing this credit seem to change frequently, and a knowledgeable accountant should be consulted to handle the details.

Depreciation

This is another subject that is best handled by securing the advice of an accountant. The principle is based on the concept that most any asset offers a gradual reduction in useful service through wear, tear and obsolescence. There are several different depreciation schedules which can be applied. Most aircraft owners would probably do best to pick the one that gives the greatest credit during the early years of ownership. Final decisions about the type and amount of depreciation to claim must be based on both, long and short-term profit projections. Depreciation must be offset against profits and is of no value if no profits are anticipated.

Deductible Expenses

Business entertainment, such as taking a customer and his wife to a resort location in your airplane, may be a perfectly legitimate attempt on your part to persuade the customer to throw more business your way. But it's the sort of thing the IRS frowns on and should be used sparingly. Do so only if you are prepared to produce reams of documents which justify it.

Educational expenses, when requested by an employer or when necessary for business, are a deductible item. This includes flight training for the owner/pilot or the professional crew. If, for instance, as an owner/pilot you live in a part of the country where the weather is IFR much of the time, then getting an instrument rating may be justified as a deductible expense. Similarly a case may be made for getting a multi-engine rating or even a jet rating if the acquisition of such an aircraft is an obvious business advantage.

It goes without saying that business-related aircraft expense, if it is justified, depends in no way on whether the aircraft is owned, leased or rented. Obviously such things as depreciation and investment tax credit apply only if the aircraft is actually owned by the taxpayer. In the case of leased aircraft, the appropriate portion of the lease payments, fuel, oil, maintenance, tiedown and the like are deductible. If the aircraft is rented, the deductions consist simply of the rental fees for business flights plus tiedown away from home base, landing fees and any fuel or oil not reimbursed by the renting FBO.

Non-Business Use of Aircraft

A number of deductions apply even if the aircraft is not used for business, and also to the non-business use of primarily business aircraft. One of these is the interest paid in the process of buying the aircraft on time. Most banks will issue a detailed statement of all interest paid at the end of each year. If these figures are not available, it is okay to divide the total interest to be paid on the loan by the number of years of the mortgage. The resultant sums will actually be too low during the early portion of the mortgage life, and too high during the last few years. Over the life of the loan it averages out satisfactorily.

Losses from theft or accident, if not covered by insurance, are deductible. These losses must be in excess of $100 in order to qualify, and not included in this category are losses caused by deterioration, corrosion and normal wear and tear.

Some states assess personal property taxes against aircraft, while others charge a state registration fee. Some do both. These payments made to the state may be deducated from the federal income tax return.

Sales taxes paid for aircraft purchases, avionics, equipment and anything else connected with the aircraft are deductible. Those using the standard sales tax tables may add these to those amounts.

Fuel taxes paid to the state are deductible unless you have applied for and received a refund. Fuel taxes paid to the federal government are, of course, not deductible. Strangely enough, for some reason the federal tax on lubricating oil is deductible by filing a separate claim on Form 4136. But this tax amounts to only 6 cents per gallon (not quart). You'd have to be using an incredible amount of oil to make this worth bothering with.

At this writing, of the 50 states, 23 do refund taxes paid on fuel used in aircraft because these taxes are "highway taxes." Since aircraft do not use highways, they should not be charged such a tax. These refunds average about six cents or so a gallon. If a lot of fuel is purchased in those 23 states, that can amount to a healthy sum, well worth the somewhat annoying paperwork connected with it. Table 7-1 shows the states and the amount of refund available from each.

Separate Aviation Corporations

In some cases businesses and even individuals form separate aviation corporations which then become the legal owner of the aircraft. These corporations then rent the aircraft to the business or individual who, usually, is either the sole owner or the major stockholder of that corporation. This type of operation is especially practical if the aircraft is used by more than one person or business, or in cases where the aircraft is operated part of the time by an FBO on a lease-back arrangement. In either instance the corporation declares its income derived from the aircraft. It is justified in declaring every cent connected with maintaining the aircraft as a deduction, no matter the type of use to which the aircraft is put by those who actually use it. If, of course, the taxes paid on possible profits by this corporation exceed the amount of deductions which the principle user of the aircraft (and major stockholder in the corporation) can claim for renting the aircraft from the corporation, this may end up defeating its purpose. Whatever the anticipated results, this type of thing can be ticklish and should not be undertaken without the assistance of a knowledgeable tax attorney.

User Taxes

Aircraft owners and pilots are currently paying a schedule of taxes that is peculiar to aviation. Officially called user *charges* rather than taxes, these consist, at this writing, of a seven cents per gallon tax on aviation fuel, plus two cents per pound for every pound of the aircraft's gross weight in excess of 2,500 pounds (in the case of turbine aircraft, 3.5 cents per pound). These charges must be considered part of the cost of owning and operating an aircraft and may be deducted just like any other expenses.

Trading Up

When the time comes to sell the airplane in order to buy another one, there are certain considerations to keep in mind. After a number of years the value of the aircraft on the company's books, due to the depreciation allowance, may just be something like one-tenth of its original value. On the other hand, the resale value of the aircraft, considering that aircraft tend to depreciate very little, often less than the prevailing rate of inflation, may be quite considerable. Thus, if the aircraft is sold outright, the company may end up with a sizable capital gain which becomes taxable. Even if the aircraft is traded for its current actual market value, it may end up being considered a taxable capital gain. The clever thing to do would be to find a dealer who is willing to take the aircraft in trade at the value at which it carried on the books of the company. And then turn around and sell the purchased aircraft at the price which would have been paid if the trade-in had been figured at its actual value.

All this may not be worth bothering with if we are talking about trading an aging Skyhawk for a Skylane. On the other hand, if we're talking about a $3 million jet which is on the company books for $300,000, but which could bring, say, $2 million on the used plane market, and the airplane to be bought is a $5 million GII, then we're talking about some real money. In the event that the dealer is

Table 7-1. Refund Amounts Available from Certain States.

State	Refund	State	Refund
Arizona	7¢	California	5¢
Delaware	9¢	Illinois	7.5¢
Iowa	7¢	Kansas	8¢
Kentucky	8.55 ¢	Louisiana	8¢
Maine	5¢	Minnesota	4 to 8.5¢
Mississippi	8¢	Missouri	7¢
Nebraska	2.5¢	Nevada	5.88 to 7.88¢
New Jersey	8¢	New Mexico	7¢
New York	8¢	North Dakota	4% of sales price is deducted from 8¢/gal refund
Rhode Island	10¢	South Dakota	1 to 3¢
Texas	5¢	Wisconsin	2¢
Wyoming	2¢		

not interested in making such a convoluted deal, there is a company called the Omni Trading Floor in Washington, D.C. which has been known to handle such transactions by itself buying the new airplane from a dealer and then making the type of deal described above. For them to be interested, it must be either a turboprop or a jet.

Finding the Right Insurance Company

Like aviation tax problems, all aviation insurance matters should be handled by an agent or company specializing in aviation. The average insurance broker and by far the greatest number of insurance companies know absolutely nothing about aviation. Using their services is likely to leave you inadequately insured at much too high a premium. There are a half dozen or so companies which specialize in aviation insurance, and their names can virtually always be found in the better aviation publications, such as *Flying* and the *AOPA Pilot*. Premiums tend to vary among the different companies and to fluctuate from year to year. A bit of shopping around is likely to save a bundle of money in the long run.

It must be understood that rates vary with the type of aircraft, the type of use to which the aircraft is put, and the experience level of the pilot(s). There are several types of insurance which have to be considered.

Liability Insurance

There are two types of liability coverage which most any business user of an aircraft will want to have. One covers any damage in terms of life or property which might occur as the result of the operation of the aircraft. The other covers death or injury of persons being carried on the airplane.

Hull Insurance

Hull insurance, as the name implies, concerns damage to the airframe, engine, components, systems, etc. There usually is one type of insurance against such damage on the ground, with the aircraft in motion and with the aircraft not in motion, and another against such damage as the result of actual flight which includes takeoff and landing. Many aircraft owners don't feel that hull insurance is worth its rather excessive cost. Unless the airplane is bought for cash or fully paid for, though, the lending institution will insist on sufficient hull insurance to cover the cost of replacement of the entire airplane—avionics, systems and all.

Miscellaneous Insurance

Then there is theft and fire insurance, insurance against acts of God, such as tornadoes, hailstorms and the like, vandalism, acts of war, and what have you. Whether most of this costs more than it is worth is something only the individual owner can decide.

It is my personal belief that the most knowledgeable man in aviation insurance is one Jay Lavenson (Harlan, Inc. 1700 Market Street, Philadelphia, PH 19103). If there is no insurance broker who specializes in aviation insurance to be found in your neighborhood, it might be worth giving Lavenson a ring or dropping him a line. If he can't help for geographic or other reasons, he is likely to know someone reasonably close to your location who can.

Chapter 8

Owner and Professional Pilots

In a great many, if not most, instances, when a company decides to use an airplane in its business, it is because the president or some other high-level executive is himself a pilot. And more often than not the initial purchase will be an airplane that he likes and feels competent to fly. From the point of view of the legalities involved, any single-engine airplane, piston twin, or turboprop can be flown by any pilot with a private pilot's license who has demonstrated his proficiency in the particular airplane in question. Of the pure-jets, to date, only one model, the Cessna Citation I SP, may be flown by a single pilot. Cessna intends to have its citation II also certificated for single-pilot operation and, as time passes, the manufacturers of some of the other jets may yet follow suit.

Pilot Error and Accidents

But legalities aside, how clever it is to have the airplane being flown by one of the company executives whose basic aim is the success of his business rather than to be a pilot? Aviation types, especially manufacturers and their representatives, like to spout all manner of statistics which can be made to prove that flying personal or business airplanes is safer than driving a car or taking a bath. But this, in fact, is a lot of baloney. If we want to be completely honest we have to accept general aviation as the most dangerous form of locomotion short of such idiotic pastimes as hang gliding or competing in the Indianapolis 500. Flying is an extremely demanding activity, one which tends to be unforgiving of inattention or sloppy performance.

Accident statistics prove time and again that the cause of the accident was pilot error. And pilot error is most often committed by someone whose mind is wrapped up in matters other than flying. This can easily happen. After all, flying long distances when the weather conditions are acceptable, the air is smooth and the wind is no noticeable factor might best be described as a terrific bore. So, we sit up there with the autopilot doing whatever work needs to be done. If we didn't have to look out for other airplanes, just in case, we might just as well go to sleep or read a book. No wonder then that our minds tend to drift to business problems, family matters, romantic fantasies or what have you.

And this is especially likely to be the case when we're on our way to an important appointement which, once we get there, will require complete attention. We'll probably be rehearsing the negotiations in advance in our mind, trying to anticipate every pitfall that might present itself. The airplane? Well, as long as the engine keeps purring happily along, there is really nothing much for us to do. Or is there? Bang! Suddenly that awful quiet. We've forgotten to switch tanks. If this happens at altitude, no problems. We switch to the other tanks, briefly turn on the electric fuel pump, and the engine will return to doing its thing. But if it had happened close to the ground, like on a long, flat approach to an airport, it could have been serious.

Or we're flying along, fat and happy, pleased that whenever we glance at it, the OBI needle remains firmly centered. Then, quite suddenly, we notice that tell-tale red flag with the word OFF. How long has that been there? We have no idea. And, as a result, we haven't the faintest notion where we are and have to scramble around to try and find some other VOR by which to relocate ourselves.

En-Route Phase of IFR Flight

Let's look at the en-route phase of IFR flight. In the old days, when ATC (air traffic control) expected us to periodically come up with the estimated time to the next checkpoint, there was rarely enough time to let one's attention drift too far. But now, with radar contact and frequently not a word from ATC for long periods of time and nothing to look at in the bargain, our thoughts can easily start to travel their own peculiar routes. The fact is that, in this situation, the intelligent thing to do is to listen attentively to everything ATC has to say, whether it concerns us or other airplanes. Time and time again ATC has been known to vector two airplanes into potential collision situations. It is always nice to know whether some other aircraft is being told to climb or descend through our altitude somewhere close by. At least then we can give them a call to make sure that they know what's going on.

What it all boils down to is the old saw about staying ahead of the airplane. As long as we accept flying as a full-time occupation while we occupy the left seat in an airplane and make sure that we're always 10 minutes or 10 miles ahead of things, we're in good shape. But let inattention cause the airplane or flight conditions to get ahead of us, and trouble will often follow.

The other consideration when an airplane is being owner-flown is the degree of proficiency which the pilot is able to maintain considering the often overriding non-aviation demands on his time. Granted, it doesn't take a whole lot of brilliance to safely and efficiently fly something like a Cessna Skylane or a Piper Dakota. These are fixed-gear airplanes with simple systems, and flying them is not particularly demanding. But few business or professional men (or women) will continue to be satisifed with such an airplane. This, then, involves the various steps up the ladder to higher and higher performance.

Tucking Away the Gear

The next step up is the ability to tuck away the gear. It's a simple operation, but one which seems to love to escape the pilot's mind at just the critical moment. There is an old saying among pilots flying retractable-gear aircraft "You've either made a belly landing or you're going to." A case in point happened some years ago at Burbank Airport in California. A doctor with some 3,000 hours in his logbook bought himself a used Mooney Ranger. He took it up for the first time, flew around a while, then came in for a landing—gear up. It took over a month to repair the airplane and, when it was finally ready, he was eager to go flying. He took it up, flew around a while, and then came in for a landing—gear up. Even the admonishment by tower controllers to "check gear down" as part of the landing clearance seems to have failed to eliminate this problem.

Need for Pilot Proficiency

But quite aside from the problem of remembering to put the gear down, the higher the performance parameters of an airplane, the faster it flies and the faster things tend to happen. In turn, the greater the need is for peak proficiency on the part of the pilot.

At first most owner pilots are loath to relinquish the left seat to someone else. But as time passes, there invariably comes the realization that an airplane, in order to justify its role as an efficient transportation machine in the overall endeavor to improve company productivity, must be flown some 400 to 500 hours a year. The average business or professional man spends about 2,000 hours a year at his work. If he's going to do all that flying himself, it means that for between 20 and 25 percent of his available time he'll be doing something other than looking after his business, namely flying the airplane. If, on the other hand, the airplane, no matter what kind it is, is being flown by someone who was hired for that purpose, then the time spent in the air can be relaxing and productive.

Pilot Responsibilities

Still, whenever the owner/pilot feels like doing some flying himself, there is no reason why the hired pilot can't move over to the right seat (Fig. 8-1). The owner/pilot can then indulge himself without having to worry about being solely responsible for the safe conduct of the flight.

Professional pilots, of course, want to be paid. As of this writing (fall 1979), pilot salaries, depending to some degree on the geographic location of the home base, range from a low of $18,000 per year for pilots flying piston singles and twins to as high as $50,000 for the captain on a two-man crew on a corporate jet. And, in addition to the salaries, there is the cost of room and board while away from home. Thus, at first glance, it may appear that the total expense involved in hiring a professional pilot will take the cost of operating an airplane right through the roof. But a rational analysis may well disprove this.

With a professional pilot on the payroll, the airplane is always available to fly anyone in the company who needs to travel, regardless of the workload at the moment of the owner/pilot himself. Furthermore it becomes the pilot's responsibility to see to it that all maintenance and minor and major repairs are performed when called for. He takes care of preparing and filing IFR flight plans and of seeing to it that the airplane is safely tied down. In advance of departure, the pilot makes sure that the airplane is preheated in the winter and ventilated in the summer, that food, drink, or whatever is on hand when needed, that the ashtrays are emptied and cleaned, and that luggage is safely placed and secured on board.

Making Flight Decisions

And there is another consideration which should not be ignored. It is the pilot's responsibility to make go/no-go decisons when adverse weather is a consideration. It is his job to decide

Fig. 8-1. Whenever the owner pilot feels like flying himself, the hired professional pilot can move over to the right seat.

whether a planned flight can be made safely, and his decision is not, and should not, be influenced by business considerations. To come up with a no-go decision is very difficult for the businessman who is about to negotiate a major merger agreement. The agreement might be in danger of being jeopardized if he doesn't get there on time. With this sort of thing on his mind, he is likely to ignore unfavorable weather reports, feeling that somehow he'll manage to get there all right. With a professional pilot it's a different story. He has the time and the obligation to check the current and expected weather conditions in all available detail. When it is obvious to him that every place within a reasonable distance of the intended destination is going to below IFR minimums at the ETA, then he simply must declare that the flight cannot be made.

Fricton Between Pilot and Businessman

This can, under certain circumstances, result in a degree of friction between the pilot and the businessman. There are cases on record where an executive has told the pilot, "If you refuse to go, you're fired." Whenever a professional pilot is engaged, it must be clearly understood by all concerned that his word in situations like this is final. No one can argue with him if it is his decision that the flight cannot take place.

The best way to accomplish this is to have it understood that the pilot's position within the company structure is somewhere in the middle-management range He is not to be looked at as simply a chauffeur, but rather as an expert professional who is being paid for his unique knowledge and capabilities.

Hiring a Pilot

Hiring that first professional pilot is not as simple as it may sound. Granted the country is full of men and women who know how to fly. A fair number of them would jump at the chance of being employed as a full-time pilot, even if the salary being offered is less than princely. But whether or not a certain pilot is the right man (woman) for the job cannot be determined by simply looking at the logbook. Maybe he's got 5,000 or 10,000 hours with a fair percentage in the type of airplane the company owns or is about to buy. But that still doesn't necessarily qualify him for the job. The fact is that you're not just looking for an experienced pilot; you're actually looking for a potential executive.

Look at it this way. Admittedly, in the beginning the primary job of the person to be hired is to fly the company airplane. With the company aviation activity still in its infancy, the scheduling will most likely be done by someone else within the company. All he has to do is take care of the airplane and be sure that he and it are ready to go when called upon. Even at this stage certain attributes in addition to piloting skills are important. The person must make a presentable appearance. He must be able to deal with upper management types and with customers without being either subservient or overbearing. He must be willing to always fly the airplane in a consecutive manner and never be tempted to execute the kind of maneuvers that tend to scare non-pilot passengers to death.

Evaluating an Applicant's Performance

If you yourself are a pilot, you can evaluate the applicant's performance in all of these areas by making a few flights with him. If you're not a pilot, you can still evaluate his personality traits. As far as his abilities as a pilot are concerned, you'll either have to take his word for them or ask some pilot friends to go up with him on a few evaluation flights. Do go along for the ride to make sure that you feel comfortable with him at the controls.

Executive Abilities

In all probability, once the company learns how to use the airplane efficiently, there will come the day when a second airplane would seem justified. That means that an additional pilot, or possibly two, may have to be hired. In fact, it will represent the beginning of the establishment of a company aviation or transportation department. If the first hired pilot is just that, a pilot but a lousy executive, you'll have a problem. Psychologically, the original pilot will expect to become the chief pilot and/or department manager. That is only logical. After all, he has seniority. But how good will he be at the increasing amount of non-flying responsibility which will more and more end up in his lap? Hiring someone else to act as chief pilot and/or department manager will create a ticklish situation. As a matter of fact, he will quite logically expect to be given the job of hiring the additional pilots, maintenance people and so on. He will expect to automatically be given the authority associated with running the flight operation.

As any one in management knows, there is nothing worse than being forced to promote someone from the ranks into a management job for which he is not suited by either temperament or ability. And it is generally true that most pilots are known to be not the greatest businessman or managers. The reason they are pilots is that they love to fly, not because they are good at shuffling papers or at telling others what to do. For this reason, when you select your first professional pilot, look for a man (or woman) whom you would feel comfortable with if he headed up one of the existing departments within the company. What you're looking for is an executive who also happens to be a good pilot.

Finding the Right Person

The next question, of course, is, where to find such a person. The average employment agencies are not likely to be of much help. And running ads in the classified sections of the local newspapers may be expected to produce a bunch of local flight instructors who've been waiting for just such an opportunity. More often than not they'll be quite young. While there is nothing wrong with youth, too much of it in the left seat of a company airplane may tend to be have a detrimental effect on the confidence level of potential passengers.

There are a number of organizations which specialize in aviation-related employment services. These people know your problems and are cognizant of what you are most probably looking for. One such is Aviation Employment Information Service, Box 240, Northport, New York 11768. Another is Rooney and Ryan, Inc., Executive Search, Box 471, Cheshire, Connecticult 06410. Both of these organizations are run by pilots and people familiar with all phases of business and corporate aviation.

Always remember that the first professional pilot you hire can make the difference between an efficient and growing flight operation, which is worth its cost, and one which simply limps along only to eventually be dismantled.

Buy First, Learn Later

As a general rule, the initial thought of acquiring a business aircraft is generated by some company executive who is already a pilot. Therefore, he is aware of the advantages to be gained from aircraft ownership. However, there are an increasing number of instances in which a company aircraft is being considered despite the fact that no one in the company knows how to fly. As has been said earlier, obtaining the services of a full-time pilot is a virtual necessity if the aircraft is to be utilized to its full potential. But that doesn't mean that it would not be advantageous in the long run if one or several members of the company are capable of flying the aircraft if the need should arise.

The usually accepted order of things is for the company president or other executive to sign up for flight instruction with a flight school. He should use the school's rental aircraft for this purpose until be obtains his private ticket. If a subsequent aircraft purchase is anticipated, this would seem to be a waste of time and money. A much more intelligent plan would be for the company president or executive to seek out the advice of a knowledgeable aircraft dealership regarding the type of aircraft which his company will eventually need. He can then purchase that aircraft and hire a professional pilot with a flight-instructor rating to fly the aircraft for the company. This person can give flight instruction to those who are interested in learning to fly.

This eliminates the cost of using a rental aircraft for some 40 or so hours at a cost of $35 or $40 per hour. Second, the new executive/pilot will be proficient in the aircraft which he will be flying instead of in some training aircraft which may be quite different and probably much more primitive. Third, the flying done as part of instruction, or at least a considerable portion of it, will consist of flights which actually have to be made for business reasons. The waste of time associated with training at a flight school is thus eliminated.

Flight instructors, many of whom ply their trade primarily to build up time in hopes of eventually landing a job as corporate or airline pilots are not toohard to find. They're always available when the offer includes a fairly decent regular salary.

Evaluating Company Needs

The only real fly in the ointment is to make sure that the airplane which the company buys is the right one for its needs. Non-pilots and even most pilots would find it difficult to make such a choice. On the other hand, the various manufacturers, especially Cessna, have people on their staff who are experts at evaluating the company's needs. They will prepare a detailed breakdown of costs in relation to utilization. In Chapter 18 we have taken one of the typical evaluations prepared by Cessna and will present it to show potential aircraft users the kind of assistance which is available for the asking. There is never any charge for this service, regardless of whether it actually results in an aircraft purchase.

Chapter 9

The Flight Department

For many small companies in which the single company airplane is being flown by the president or some other high-level executive, the idea of talking about a flight department may, on the surface, seem ridiculous. "Flight department? What for? When I need to go some place I go, period, It's as simple as that." But is it?

Travel Coordinator

What happens is that the six-place airplane is flown most of the time with five empty seats. Why? Nobody else in the company, some of whom having a need to travel to the same destination or at least in the same general direction, knew of the fact that the company airplane was going that way. As a result, others in the company used their cars, or bought airline tickets and ended up wasting not only time but also money.

An actual flight department is not necessarily needed. What is needed is just one person who, possibly in addition to a variety of other duties, acts as a clearing point for all transportation needs and requests. This could be the boss's secretary or anyone else in the company. It must be someone who has the time, inclination and intelligence to be able to figure the advantages and disadvantages of one type of travel over another in terms of time and cost. When such a person has been given the responsibility for all company travel, then each company executive or employee must check with him or her as soon as the date and itinerary for a business trip becomes known. Thus, when the president knows that next Wednesday he has to go to Middletown and on Friday to Centerville, he gives this information along with expected takeoff time and the time of return to the travel desk.

The travel coordinator may already know that someone else in the company, be it a salesman, engineer or what have you, has plans to be in either of those cities on, say, Thursday. The coordinator will then contact that person to ascertain whether he or she can change the appointment to Wednesday (or Friday), in which case he can travel on the company aircraft at no additional cost to the company. The coordinator might even contact various department heads to find out if there are any not yet announced plans for travel in that general direction. If so, the availability of the aircraft (which, if necessary, could make an intermediate stop to drop off or pick up a passenger) might cause some indefinite travel plans to be firmed up to coincide with the announed schedule.

This is a miniature version of what happens or should happen in even the largest corporations with their multi-jet fleets. Airplanes and their operation, no matter the type and size, are simply too expensive to own and operate to be used as some type of Royal Barge by only the company president and his most intimate pals. Any company with stockholders and the attendant requirement to disclose profits and losses cannot afford to seriously under-utilize such an expensive business tool. Thus, as the company's aviation activity grows, first by trading up to a faster, more efficient (and expensive) airplane, and then possibly to two or more airplanes, it becomes increasingly important that all business transportation, be it people or freight, be coordinated at one central point. At this point it is no longer the sort of thing that can be handled by a secretary as an adjunct to other duties. It has now reached the stage of a full-fledged transportation department with a transportation manager, a secretary in charge of scheduling, a group of pilots (and copilots), and one or several expert maintenance people.

Pilots as Transportation Managers

It is not at all unusual that the first professional pilot hired by a company on its climb from that original owner-flown Skylane to the first turboprop or jet will end up being the manager of the aviation or transportation department (Fig. 9-1). Here the distinction in terminology becomes important. If the department is known within the company as the "aviation department," persons with transportation needs may hesitate to contact the department when the logical mode of transportation quite obviously appears to be one other than a company airplane. On the other hand, if is known as the "transportation department," then the implication quite obviously is that all matters relating to transportation by any means what-soever should be handled by that department. Whether or not placing all transportation responsibilities on the shoulders of that first-hired professional pilot is a good idea depends largely on the type of person involved.

Good pilots are not necessarily good managers. Many a pilot is much too enamored of the act of actually handling the controls of an airplane. He likely will not be good at spending the better part of his life behind a desk. On the other hand, the department manager, whether pilot or not, must know about aviation, the performance capabilities and limitations of the aircraft, the effects of weather, costs of operation, maintenance considerations, requirements for recurrent flight-crew training and so on. The type of individual who runs the aviation/transportation department can be largely instru-mental in making it either successful or causing it to be an expen-sive appendage, hard to justify.

Availability of Aircraft

The degree to which the company aircraft should be available to persons at varying levels within the company hierarchy is a decision which must be made by management and then im-plemented by the department manager. There can be no doubt that companies which let just about anyone with a need to travel have access to company aircraft turn out to be those in which the cost of travel per passenger mile is the lowest. This doesn't mean that the company president, who is flying one of his customers to an important destination, must necessarily be surrounded by a bunch of roughnecks in dirty overalls on their way to a construction site. Obviously, there are times when privacy en route is justified and important. But more often than not, there is no real reason why most or all of the seats in the aircraft couldn't be filled, assuming that several people have the need to travel in the same general direction.

Running such a department requires a great deal of diplomacy and tact. It is unavoidable that from time to time persons with a need to travel have to be refused a seat on company aircraft. They may have to be bumped after having made a reservation because some emergency situation has arisen. Also, there are times when weather or the need for some unscheduled maintenance forces cancellation of a flight. No one, but no one, and that includes the president and the chairman of the board, should be in a position to even attempt to countermand a chief pilot's no-go decision. The

Fig. 9-1. Aviation departments may consist of a mixed fleet of fixed and rotary-wing aircraft.

chief pilot must be the pilot in command of all company aviation activity. It is his judgement and no one else's that decides whether a flight can be made safely or whether it needs to be postponed or canceled. If the chief pilot is also the department manager, then it is his responsibility to confront the boss with the bad news. If the department is managed by some person other than the chief pilot, he can give his evaluation of the situation to that manager, who then has the unpleasant task of telling the chairman of the board that he can't go.

Department Responsibilities

The areas of responsibility for such a department include everything that has to do with the operation and maintenance of the company aircraft: scheduling, keeping records of all fixed and variable costs, flights made, number of passengers carried, distances flown, hours flown, the hiring and firing of pilots and copilots as well as maintenance personnel. If it is a total transportation department it will also be responsible for keeping records of all other related expenses, etc., when alternate modes of transportation are being used by company people. In addition, the conscientious department manager will conduct a continuous low-profile public relations campaign within the company. He must make sure that everyone who might even marginally be entitled to make use of the aircraft is aware of their availability and capabilities. Furthermore he should, at frequent intervals, evaluate the suitability of the company aircraft relative to the travel requirements of the company. It is not at all unusual for the profile of the overall travel activity to change.

Fig. 9-2. The Learjet, this one a model 28/29, is ideal for missions in the 1,000-mile-plus range.

Thus, a company which has been operating a Citation or Learjet primarily for transporting upper-echelon personnel to destinations 500 or more miles away from home base may suddenly find it has an urgent need to take engineering or workforce personnel to closer but more inaccessible destination on a regular basis (Fig. 9-2).

An entirely different type of airplane may be needed. If there is a convenient landing strip available, a medium piston twin or even a high performance single may be the right vehicle (Figs. 9-3 and 9-4). If the location is such that landing fixed-wing aircraft would be difficult, it may require considering the acquisition of a helicopter (Fig. 9-5). Either way, it is the job of the department manager to evaluate the situation and to determine what type of

Fig. 9-3. A medium twin is useful for shorter distances when a nearby airstrip is available.

Fig. 9-4. A high performance single may also do that job effectively.

aircraft could be used most efficiently. Then he confronts top management with a complete proposal. If the need for such a second aircraft is limited in terms of time, it may be advisable to lease such an airplane for a given number of months or years. If the situation or similar situations are expected to last for a long time, it would probably pay to purchase the extra airplane.

There may even be times when the vast majority of the travel needs could better and more economically be performed by a turboprop or a cabin-class piston twin. This, too, should then be brought to the attention of top management which can then decide whether the status symbol value attached to the jet is worth the extra cost, or whether it would be wiser to get rid of the jet in exchange for one or possibly several less expensive airplanes.

Scheduling

Scheduling is one of the more complicated problems facing the aviation/transportation department. Some companies that have need for large numbers of people to travel frequently between fixed

Fig. 9-5. When no convenient airstrip is nearby, a helicopter, such as this S-76 Spirit, may be the better choice.

locations have solved the problem by instituting regularly scheduled flights of one or several aircraft. They then operate much like a private airline. Departure days of the week and times of day are set for each aircraft and each location, and people with a need to travel simply make reservations. This system was pioneered by old Henry Ford, who used a fleet of Ford Trimotors to conduct flights on regular schedules between his various plants in the 1920s.

When the development of the original Lear Jet inaugurated the age of the corporate jet, the Rexall Drug Company in Los Angeles placed the first order for a fleet of those Lear Jet 23s, using them on regularly scheduled flights which crisscrossed the country from coast to coast. Rexall also pioneered the idea that the company aircraft should be available to anyone in the company on a first-come-first-served basis whenever empty seats were available. Another company which uses this system is Xerox, which flies a Gulfstream I on a regular daily schedule between certain company locations in a strictly airline type operation. In each case the company has other aircraft which are available for on-demand type of service.

The on-demand scheduling is more complicated. It requires a constant analysis and awareness of individual travel needs relative to the available aircraft. This is necessary to avoid unnecessary deadheading or making several trips where careful planning could have combined these trips into one with slight detours or inter-mediate stops.

Transportation Charging

Regardless of the type of scheduling used by the company, there is always the question of who should be charged with what. Most often accountants or comptrollers would prefer to have each department or individual charged with the actual cost of the trans-portation in company aircraft that is being used by the department or individual. But this actual cost, without making allowance for time saved and the many other intangible advantages, tends to be quite high. Department managers and individuals who have to worry about staying within certain given annual budgets will often balk at such expense, resulting in the under-utilization of the airplane. If each department or individual is to be charged for the use of the airplane, it would seem more sensible to simply charge a fixed per-passenger-mile fee, set to compare favorably or reason-ably close to the per-passenger-mile cost involved in using alternate means of travel. In such a case there will be a loss, representing the aviation costs not thus covered, which then becomes part of the regular company overhead, charged to each department on the normal proportionate basis. This system encourages aircraft utilization and, in fact, reduces the actual cost per passenger mile in the long run.

Some companies have decided that it is preferable to simply lump all aviation-related costs into the overall overhead figure. They make no direct charge to the departments or individuals using the aircraft. This, too, tends to encourage aircraft utilization and is probably ideal for relatively small companies. It may prove impractical for large corporations with all manner of subsidiaries who have access to the airplanes.

No two companies use the exact same systems. All appear to have an efficient and well-run aviation department, no matter whether we are talking about one airplane or a fleet. The aviation activity, in the long run, is an important company adjunct, responsible for measurable increases in productivity.

Chapter 10

Instrument Rating

In recent years there has been a somewhat less than subtle campaign by the FAA and much of the aviation industry intended to make us feel that, unless we are instrument rated, we are somehow unclean. Considering the constantly increasing restrictions on the use of certain portions of the airspace, not to mention the number of VFR pilots who annually insist on flying into IFR conditions only to end up hitting a mountain, spinning out, or otherwise committing suicide (or, in the case of passengers, murder), there may be a considerable degree of justification for it. Still, not everyone needs an instrument rating. Figuring the cost and time involved in getting one, it might be worthwhile to analyze who does and who does not.

Instrument Proficiency

Let's emphasize the fact that there is a difference between an instrument rating and instrument proficiency. An instrument rating is a piece of paper that gives the holder the legal right to conduct flights from takeoff to landing under IFR conditions, including flying approaches to published minimums in high-density terminal areas. Instrument proficiency refers to the degree to which the pilot is actually capable of conducting instrument operations in the aircraft which he happens to be flying at the time. For instance, a 10,000-hour airline captain may be eminently qualified to fly an instrument approach to 200-and-a-half at some familiar major terminal in a 747 equipped with dual or tripple everything and assisted by a copilot. His rating also gives him the right to fly that same approach without copilot in a Cherokee or Skyhawk, equipped with a bare minimum of avionics appropriate to the particular approach. Chances are, unless he has spent much of his spare time in light aircraft, his proficiency will be less than adequate for the task at hand.

Instrument proficiency, then, consists of a variety of interfacing factors. First, and above all, is the ability to fly and control the aircraft by reference to instruments alone. Second is to navigate with a reasonable degree of precision, using the avionics available in the aircraft being flown. Third is a familiarity with the rules, regulations and procedures relating to instrument flight in general, and the specific approach to be flown in particular. And last, but certainly not least, is an acceptable amount of recent experience.

Reasons for Knowing Instrument Flying

Let's take first things first. No matter whether or not you are instrument rated or intend one day to be instrument rated, the ability to fly and control the aircraft by reference to instruments alone is an absolute necessity for anyone wishing to make sufficient use of his aircraft to justify owning it. Not only does most night flying require operating by reference to instruments rather than visual cues, but huge portions of today's airspace are frequently saturated with haze which, though technically VFR, produces conditions in which visual references become vague and unreliable.

In addition, it is always possible, though no weather is ever capable of catching up with a moving aircraft, that you misinterpret the degree of severity of cloud, haze or fog conditions. This can cause you to fly into an IFR situation that will necessitate a 180-degree turn on instruments in order to safely get back to where things are VFR. The minimum amount of instrument practice that is part of the private pilot curriculum today is not enough. Whenever safely possible, instrument flying should be practiced so that instrument readings can be interpreted instantly. That most difficult of the psychological problems associated with instrument flight, the ability to believe in the instrument readings and to ignore false sensations generated by the balance mechanism in the inner ear, requires a conscious effort.

Navigating by instruments is something most of us do practically all the time anyway. This may cause us to think of it as a simple routine matter. And, during the en-route phase of most any flight it is just that, routine. But when it comes to flying a VOR, an ADF approach or, for that matter, entering a holding pattern, the problem of intercepting the appropriate radial and flying an exact direction for a predetermined distance becomes an exercise in precision to which the average VFR pilot is totally unaccustomed.

Again, practicing precision during routine VFR flights, staying exactly on the center of the airway and slicing the VORs in half as we pass over them, is valuable training.

Rules and Regulations

Rules, regulations and procedures are a different story. While important when on an IFR flight plan, most are meaningless to the VFR pilot. Their study is simply one of the less exhilarating activities that are part and parcel of preparing for the tests involved in obtaining an instrument rating.

The need for recent experience, while immensely important when faced with one of the trickier IFR situations is ignored by a great percentage of instrument rated pilots who must use their aircraft as an efficient transportation machine in the conduct of their business or profession. It goes without saying that what we do frequently tends to become second nature. Adequate recent experience simply reduces the sweaty palm syndrome when things get more hectic than usual. The reason that so many instrument rated business pilots are loath to file IFR under VFR conditions is that much of it is a pain in the neck. The idea of working out the details of an IFR flight plan, filing it at least a half an hour ahead of departure, copying a clearance which frequently bears little resemblance to what was filed, examining and repeating this clearance and then following it or subsequent amendments transmitted by ATC (Air Traffic Control) is hard work. Often you waste considerably more time and fuel than by simply taking off VFR, heading in the right direction and then letting the autopilot take you to your destination. The FARs (Federal Aviation Regulations) of course, stipulate a given number of hours and approaches that must have been flown IFR during the preceding six months in order to be legal. This stipulation is both unenforceable and generally ignored by non-professional pilots.

Three Questions

Now let's get back to the premise of this chapter to be or not to be instrument rated. In trying to analyze the potential value of the instrument rating to the individual pilot owner, let's first look at the answers to three questions:

■ Is the prevailing weather at home base and along the routes most frequently flown such that VFR operations are often marginal, dangerous or quite impossible, resulting in postponements, delays or cencellations?

■ Does the aircraft at hand have the appropriate amount of avionics and instrumentation as well as adequate range? If not, is it economically possible to either trade up or add to the instrumentation and/or range of the existing aircraft?

■ Does the pilot/owner have the time and money to indulge in the amount of practice necessary to become and stay proficient?

Geography and Weather

Relative to the first question, the answer should be easy. If home base is a place like Phoenix, Albuquerque or El Paso and most of the flying is done to Denver, Salt Lake City or Boise, then the need to file instruments is likely to occur less than six times a year. Even then, IFR conditions rarely stick around for more than a few hours at a time. In addition, the MEAs (minimum enroute altitudes) in mountain areas are generally so high as to make them impractical for the average light aircraft without oxygen.

On the other hand, aircraft owners based in Los Angeles, Memphis, Chicago, Seattle or anywhere in the northeastern United States are faced with days upon days of solid overcasts, frequent ground fog during the early morning hours, air pollution and related phenomena that produce prolonged instrument conditions. This reduces the ability to adhere to some sort of reliable schedule while staying VFR. The temptation and frequent necessity to file IFR, if only to get to VFR conditions on top or to descend through the overcast to conditions of ample ceiling and visibility below, would seem to make an instrument rating necessary.

Money

The second consideration is largely one of money. Not all aircraft are adequate for hard instrument flying. The overriding consideration should be range. In order to be legal it must be possible to reach the destination and then an alternate, say, 100 miles distant, and still have a 45-minute reserve of fuel on board. This does not even include one or two missed approaches before deciding to head for the alternate. An aircraft with VFR range of 500 miles is suddenly reduced to an effective IFR range of only 300 miles or less, certainly not a very comfortable feeling.

Proper Equipment

Adequate instrumentation should be next on the list. Granted, the rules require only that "instrumentation adequate to the in-

Fig. 10-1. Instrument panel of a Cessna Skylane, adequately equipped for IFR operations.

tended approach" be on board, but flying IFR with a bare minimum of radio equipment and without an autopilot can easily turn into a hair-raising experience. Quite aside from the basic need for reliable navcom radios, preferably in duplicate, these days a transponder and an encoding altimeter are required when one must operate to, from or through TCAs (terminal control areas), or when one wants to cruise above 12,500 feet. In addition, a glide slope, market beacon and an ADF (automatic direction finder), perferably digital, increase the IFR flexibility of the aircraft by a meaningful margin (Fig. 10-1 through 10-4). Further, a reliable autopilot would seem to be a must. At least it can be depended upon to fly the airplane through bumps and turbulence while the pilot studies approach plates, copies amended clearances, or is otherwise preoccupied by the dozens of chores that frequently crop up when one least expects them.

A DME, though not a necessity, does help to make life much easier. And once a DME is on hand, the next step is RNAV, which has proved in recent years to be vastly more useful than was originally anticipated. For those who can afford the cost, a flight director, preferably coupled to the autopilot, is certainly one of the greatest aids a pilot can ask for.

Load-Carrying Capability

One parameter that is frequently overlooked when analyzing the IFR capability of an aircraft is its load-carrying capability, rate of climb and service ceiling. The combination of these determines the ability of the aircraft to climb through icing conditions to higher altitudes without picking up more ice along the way than it can handle. Icing in clouds is one of the major enemies of the lightplane IFR pilot, but it is virtually impossible to operate IFR with any regularity without encountering ice from time to time. The load-carrying capability, if adequate, means that one can pick up an inch or so of ice without having to worry that the stall speed increases to the point where it approaches the maximum speed available with the somewhat deformed airfoil. An acceptable rate of climb makes it possible to climb through 1,000 or 2,000 feet of icing to colder or warmer areas above fast enough to get there before too much ice has been formed. An adequately high service ceiling permits one to operate above the worst of the weather much of the time where icing is no longer a problem.

Pilot Discipline

The third question we posed is one only the pilot/owner himself can answer. Does he feel that he can shut out the demands and preoccupations of his business and devote his full attention to the task posed by operating IFR? Is he disciplined enough to set himself personal minimums appropriate to his proficiency (and higher than those officially listed on the approach plates)? Can he religiously stick to those personal minimums in the face of tempta-

Fig. 10-2. The instrument panel of a Cessna Turbo Centurion with RNAV and autopilot.

Fig. 10-3. The instrument panel of a Cessna Golden Eagle with RNAV, flight director and weather radar.

tion to try for lower ones when it means getting to the desired destination? Does he do much of his flying at the tailend of a day filled with hard and tiring work, meaning that his abilities may be impaired by fatigue?

One additional consideration affects primarily those pilots who habitually operate rented aircraft. Operating IFR is difficult enough when it is done in an aircraft with which the pilot is thoroughly familiar. Add to it even a minor degree of unfamiliarity, such as is unavoidable when flying rented aircraft, and complications tend to pile up too fast for comfort. Minor variations in panel layout, differences in the response to control input, and even such seemingly meaningless items as the ability to effectively control the degree of ventilation or heat can have a detrimental effect on the pilot's performance.

Exam Difficulty

In considering getting an instrument rating in the light of all the above, it must be remembered that we are talking about an investment in terms of training alone of some $5,000 or more, not to mention the time involved. It is the general consensus that the instrument written exam is by far the most difficult of the various FAA tests. The fact remains that, once having put school and college behind us by some years or even decades, we find it difficult to reorient our thinking into the type of channels which are a prerequisite for success in passing a rigid test.

Discussions with non-IFR-rated high-time pilots usually elicit such statements as: "I tried to take that written once and flunked, and I just don't feel up to trying it again. And, without it, what's the point of wasting all that time and money involved in taking the flight training?" What this indicates is the need for a relatively painless and foolproof way to take and pass the IFR written in advance of the actual flight training. Then, with the problem of successfully passing the test out of the way, one can concentrate on the flight portion of the instruction at a schedule which least interferes with normal business activities. There can be no doubt about the fact that the IFR written test has very little relevance to practical instrument flying. A student passing it with a score of 90 or better is likely to know all manners of thoroughly forgettable nomenclature and theory without having the faintest idea of what it means to actually operate in the IFR environment.

Cram Courses

For this very reason, those of use whose minds are normally occupied with the mundane problems of business, family and social life would be best advised to consider the cram courses offered by organizations such as Accelerate Pilot Training (APT) of Santa Barbara, California, which conducts such cram courses on weekends in various cities around the country. These courses make little pretense of teaching instrument flying. Their one sole purpose is to force-feed the students all the information necessary to pass the test, period. They involve two very full days of instruction and the taking of several practice tests which are designed to get them accustomed and attuned to dealing with the kind of test that the FAA will throw at them. On the morning of the third day, arrangements have been made to take the actual test. Anyone of reasonable intelligence, willing to devote all day and all evening of Saturday and Sunday to the subject, will successfully pass the test on Monday.

Proper Study Habits

Ideally, students should check into the motel or hotel in which the instruction is being given, even if it happens to be located in or

Fig. 10-4. The instrument panel of a Beech Super King Air 200 with just about everything.

near their home town. It simply is not possible to absorb all that information, go home and, surrounded by a wife, children, the telephone and TV, to study and effectively complete the homework which includes, on the evening of the first day, one of the practice tests. It requires complete immersion. Staying at the motel, ignoring the bar and beckoning TV set will help to keep the mind concentrating on the purpose of this whole exercise. These cram courses range in cost from around $100 to $150. They are guaranteed, meaning that a student who flunks the test can retake the instruction and test free of charge over and over again until he finally makes it. Having passed the hurdle of the written test tends to make the subsequent flight instruction easy and enjoyable by comparison, and it may actually reduce the number of hours needed to finally get that sought-after ticket.

Summary

To be instrument rated and proficient is certainly worthwhile and will tend to increase the utility of the aircraft. But it is not the absolute necessity that some would have us believe. If an analysis of the business requirements, the aircraft itself, the travel needs and the financial ability of the owner/pilot is positive, then he should start working on his rating tomorrow. But if at least some of the answers are negative, it might be better to accept the limits imposed by VFR and to adjust the schedules and flight needs accordingly.

But don't try and have your cake and eat it, too. In other words, don't be one of those characters who figures: "I can handle this bird on instruments, so, the heck with ATC. I'll just plow up there through the overcast until I come out in VFR conditions on top, and no one will be the wiser." Granted, you'll probably get away with it and the chances of running into another aircraft are relatively small. Still, you simply don't have the right to endanger the lives of those in another aircraft, even if you don't care about your own. If you don't have an IFR rating, but you feel that you're that good on instruments, then at least have the decency to call ATC and file. Unless you sound like a total amatuer, ATC won't ask whether or not you're rated. At least you'll become part of the system, making it possible for the controllers to keep you and other traffic safely separated.

Chapter 11

Wings or Wheels

Bill McCoy is a salesman for a machine tool manufacturing company with headquarters in Hillsboro near Portland, Oregon. He has been with the company since it was founded some twenty years ago, and his territory includes the 10 western states. For years he used to cram the trunk and back seat of his Oldsmobile full of samples, sales literature, price lists and catalogs. He spent long evening and night hours driving from city to city in order to spend his days making calls on potential customers.

Leaving Ground for Air

One night, sometime between eleven o'clock and midnight, he dozed off at the wheel and ended up in a ditch. Luckily neither he nor the car were seriously injured or damaged, but it was then and there that he decided that there must be a better way to get around. The trouble was that the airlines didn't go to many of the places on his itinerary. Even where airline service was available, the schedules were such that he'd end up wasting an unconscionable amount of time.

He discussed the problem with friends and someone suggested that he learn to fly and buy himself an airplane. It was an idea which had never occurred to him. Granted, like everyone else he had seen little airplanes scooting around in the sky. Somehow he had never thought about the fact that those were real people, just like himself, who were flying them.

McCoy went to Hillsboro Airport, talked to someone at the first flight school he came across, and 15 minutes later he was in the air. In another 15 minutes he was hooked. To make a long story short, he signed up for lessons, got his private license, and bought himself a used Cessna 172.

At first, his employer was not exactly ecstatic when told of this new development. He was worried about company liability in the event of an accident. Also, he was convinced that Bill's expense accounts would double or triple because of the higher cost of operating the airplane. But Bill agreed to carry his own liability insurance and, initially at least, to figure his expenses based on what it would have cost to travel by car. At that point he wasn't at all certain that this would end up being a financially advantageous deal for him. He figured, though, that it was better than getting himself killed on the highway.

Flight Plan

Soon it was time for him to get back on the road. He carefully preplanned his proposed flight in great detail, the kind of detail which all of us indulge in during the early stages of our flying careers, before we have accumulated sufficient experience to take it all somewhat more casually.

The planned flight looked like this:

Portland, OR to Olympia, WA—75 nm, 45 min;
Olympia, WA to Seattle, WA—36 nm, 22 min;
Seattle, WA to Ephrata, WA—118 nm, 1:11 hrs;
Ephrata, WA to Spokane, WA—74 nm, 45 min;
Spokane, WA to Missoula, MT—153 nm, 1:32 hrs;
Missoula, MT to Butte, MT—75 nm, 45 min;
Butte, MT to Billings, MT—172 nm, 1:44 hrs;
Billings, MT to Cody, WY—73 nm, 44 min;
Cody, WY to Casper, WY—159 nm, 1:36 hrs;
Casper WY to Denver, CO—212 nm, 2:08 hrs;
Denver, CO to Colorado Springs, CO—55 nm, 33 min;
Colorado Springs, CO to Santa Fe, NM—236 nm, 2:22 hrs;
Santa Fe, NM to Farmington, NM—141 nm, 1:25 hrs;
Farmington, NM to Las Vegas, NV—350 nm, 3:30 hrs;
Las Vegas, NV to Salt Lake City, UT—330 nm, 3:18 hrs;
Salt Lake City, UT to Boise, ID—250 nm, 2:30 hrs;
Boise, ID to Portland, OR—300 nm, 3:00 hrs.

McCoy figured therefore that his total flying time would add up to 28:10 hours during which time he would cover some 2,817 nm. Assuming an average fuel consumption of 7.5 gph (gallons per hour), he would be burning 211.25 gallons of fuel and would probably have to add some three quarts of oil. Because of the deal with his employer according to which he would be charged the equivalent in automobile expenses, he then sat down to figure out the mileages involved. It added up to 4,138 road miles (3,598 nautical miles), meaning that, with an average fuel consumption in his Olds at 18 mpg, he would be using 230 gallons of premium gasoline, plus, probably, four quarts of oil.

All this took place some years ago when things, especially fuel, were considerably cheaper. In order to make this meaningful in terms of today's prices, let's assume that the avgas would cost McCoy $1.20 per gallon while the fuel for his car would average around $1.00 per gallon. Thus, he would be spending $232.50 for fuel in his airplane, plus another $3 for oil. The automobile would be costing him $230 for gas plus approximately $5 for oil. So what we are talking about here is that the airplane would cost him 50 cents more than the car.

Airplane Trip Details

But, and here comes the rub, by using the airplane, assuming two hours per sales call, hours which would have to be between 9 a.m. and 5 p.m., he would be able to break it down in this manner. He will have to take off from Hillsboro at around 8 a.m. on Monday morning which will get him to Olympia at about 8:45 a.m. He will see his customer between nine and 11 a.m. and be back in the air by 11:15 a.m. This will get him to Seattle shortly before noon. He will, of course, have called ahead and made an appointment for 1:00 p.m. This will give him time for a quick lunch. By 3:15 p.m. he'll be back in his airplane and will be landing in Ephrata by 4:25 p.m. or so. By calling ahead he can probably arrange to meet his customer there shortly before 5:00 p.m. People are generally rather cooperative when they are told that their visitors are arriving by private airplane. McCoy will still be able to go on to Spokane and check into a motel.

The next day he will take care of his business in Spokane the first thing in the morning and be on his way by, say, 11:10 a.m. That will get him to Missoula by about 12:45 p.m. and, by cutting his lunch hour short, he'll be able to make his sale by 1:30 p.m. He'll then be back in the air by about 3:30 and will be landing in Butte by 4:15 p.m. Again, by calling ahead he can most probably arrange to see his man there, possibly by offering to buy him a drink. (He himself will have a Virgin Mary or some such, considering that he'll still be doing some flying that day). He will then take off again and fly to Billings where he'll be spending the night.

In Billings Bill McCoy might be lucky to arrange for a breakfast meeting at, say, 8:00 a.m., which will get him back into the air by 10:00 a.m. He will reach Cody by 10:45 a.m. in time for a pre-lunch meeting there. By 1:15 p.m., having munched a quick sandwich, he'll then be on his way to Casper, landing there at about 2:50 p.m. The meeting there will be the last of that day, but afterwards there is still time for him to take off again and fly on to Denver. He would spend the night there.

It's now Thursday. Again he will have arranged for an early breakfast meeting which will make it possible for him to be at his next stop in Colorado Springs before lunch. Then he goes to Santa Fe still early enough to conduct his business there. Having experienced a pretty full day, McCoy will decide to spend a leisurely evening in Santa Fe and to take off at the crack of dawn the next morning.

On Friday he'll get to Farmington in time for an early appointment. By 10:30 a.m. he is again on his way, this time to Las Vegas, Nevada. That's a long flight and he'll get to Las Vegas by 1:00 p.m., having gained one hour along the way because of the time change. The meeting there lasts until about 3:30 or so, which doesn't matter because there is no way for him to get to Salt Lake City during business hours. Salt Lake City is again in the Mountain Time zone, thus causing him to lose an hour along the way. But the fellow in Salt Lake City is an old customer. When Bill calls him to find out if he can see him on Saturday, he suggests that they have dinner that night instead. Thus, arriving in Salt Lake at about 8:00 p.m. Mountain Time, his customer meets him at the airport and they go out to dinner and conduct their business over a good steak. Meanwhile Bill has also called his customer in Boise who has agree to meet him on Saturday morning.

So, on Saturday, he leaves Salt Lake City at about 7:30 a.m. and, gaining the hour back as he crosses again into the Pacific Time zone, he arrives in Boise at 9:00 a.m. By 11:00 a.m., he had made his sale and after a cup of coffee and a sandwich, he's in the air shortly after noon. He then lands back home at Hillsboro around 3:00 p.m. and, with his briefcase full of orders, he can spend a relaxed Saturday afternoon and Sunday with his wife and children.

Costs

In addition to the $235.50 for fuel and oil, the trip has cost him five nights in a motel at an average of $35 per night, totaling $175. His meals, at an average of $20 per day for five and a half days, have come to $110. In addition he has paid $16.25 for tiedowns plus $78.12 for various taxis and car rentals. The total cost of the trip amounts to $614.87. To be realistic, the reserves for major overhaul, insurance and other fixed expenses should be added to this figure. These costs amount to approximately $6.17 per hour, or a total for the 28.17 hours of flying of $173.81, making it a grand total of $788.68.

The Same Trip by Car

Now let's look at the same trip by car. To be fair, despite the prevailing 55-mph speed limit, let's give Bill McCoy the benefit of the doubt and figure the automobile at an average speed of 60 miles.

On Monday morning, leaving an hour and a half earlier, he will be ready for his meeting in Olympia at the same time. The trip into Seattle with the Tacoma and Seattle traffic will take at least an hour and a half. His meeting there will be over by mid-afternoon and he'll be on his way to Ephrata, a distance of 159 miles. Let's be kind and say he gets there in two hours and 40 minutes and, by calling ahead, he's arranged for a late afternoon meeting. Thus far, he has managed to cram in just about as much as he would have by using the plane. With the meeting finished he now gets back on the road and drives the 121 miles to Spokane where he'll spend the night.

On Tuesday the first meeting in Spokane is successfully concluded at about 10:30 a.m. He's now on his way to Missoula. That's a distance of 198 miles and it takes him three hours and 20 minutes to get there. By skipping lunch he'll be able to have his meeting there at 3:00 p.m. He's losing one hour along the way as he moves into another time zone. Shortly after 4:40 p.m. he is back on the road and on his way to Butte, 112 miles. By the time he gets there it's too late to do any business, so he checks into a motel.

On Wednesday morning he is up bright and early for a meeting and then is back in his car by 10:45 a.m. The trip from Butte to Billings covers a distance of 249 miles which takes him four hours and 10 minutes, plus a half hour for lunch. This gets him into Billings at around 3:30 p.m., still in time to conduct his business. But that's it. So he has a leisurely meal in Billings and then drives the 106 miles to Cody where he checks in for the night.

It's now Thursday. His morning meeting is over by 10:00 and he's on the road to drive the 302 miles to Casper. That's a good five-hour drive plus a half hour for lunch, getting him to his destination at 3:30 p.m., still in time for one more appointment. With that out of the way, a question arises. Having already driven five hours, should he attempt to drive another 284 miles to Denver? Bill is pretty well beat so he decides to relax in Casper for the evening.

On Friday morning he leaves at 5:30 a.m. and arrives in Denver at 10:15 a.m. After his meeting there he stops for a quick lunch and then goes on to Colorado Springs which only takes an hour and a half. His business there is concluded by 3:45. Despite the early four-plus hours of driving, he gets back into his car and starts on the 321-mile drive to Santa Fe. By the time he finally gets there it's after 10:00 p.m. After a quick hamburger he falls into his motel bed, half dead.

Finishing the Automobile Trip

Santa Fe is not a place in which people take kindly to doing business on Saturdays. He decides that he might as well relax and spend a comfortable weekend there.

On Monday morning, promptly at 9:00 a.m., he finally has his meeting with his Santa Fe customer and by 10:30 he's on his way to Farmington. There is no direct road, so the distance adds up to 205 miles, which takes him just under three and a half hours. At 2:00 he meets with his client and at 3:45 p.m., having gulped down a quick and not very satisfying lunch, he is on his way to Las Vegas. That's 549 miles or over nine hours of driving, not counting stops for fuel and food. Though he will be gaining an hour along the way, it would still be around 2:00 a.m. by the time he'd get there. He figures that he'll simply drive until he gets too tired and then stay somewhere along the way. That somewhere would probably turn out to be Flagstaff.

His initial thought is to leave Flagstaff very early. Realizing that the next leg, Las Vegas to Salt Lake City, will involve another 458 miles of driving, though, plus the loss of an hour due to the difference in time zones, he decides that it doesn't make much difference. He therefore leaves Flagstaff in time to get to Las Vegas around lunch. After a bite to eat and losing six quarters in an uncooperative slot machine, he makes his sale and then heads north, arriving in Salt Lake some time between 10:30 and 11:00 p.m. Mountain Time.

His meeting will last until about 10:30 a.m. after which he'll be on his way to Boise, 338 miles. Gaining the hour back while en route, he will then arrive in Boise about 3:00 p.m., early enough to conclude his business there. He will likely have an early dinner and, anxious to get home, will start driving by 6:00 p.m. or so. The distance to Portland is 468 miles, so he'll be getting home by about 2:00 a.m. on Thursday.

Costs Comparison

Since it is reasonable to assume that Bill's arrangement with his employer calls for payment for the use of his car in terms of so much per mile, say 17 cents, his expense account will now look like this, with 4,138 miles at 0.17 totaling $703.46. Nine nights in a motel at $35 totals $315. Ten days of food etc. at $20 comes to $200 making a grand total of $1,218.46.

As it turned out, Bill McCoy actually made a profit of $429.78 by using the airplane. It is not surprising that, on subsequent trips, the employer opted for paying the expenses based on using the airplane rather than the automobile.

Chapter 12

The Care Of Passengers

Whenever a company acquires an airplane, it will sooner or later be used to carry customers to company headquarters or to transport other non-pilot passengers (Fig. 12-1). Whenever this happens; it is important that the person flying the airplane is aware of the somewhat queasy feeling which non-pilots tend to have about traveling in a light aircraft. This is especially true when the airplane involved is a single or a light twin.

Steep banks, which we pilots take for granted, often cause passnegers to get all shook up. Even light turbulence will tend to upset the unaccustomed stomach. Passengers often get spooked by all that radio chatter, much of which they usually are unable to understand and some of which they may actually misunderstand. On the other hand, the kinds of situations which may bother us as pilots—low visibilities, moonless nights, lowering ceilings or even the sudden appearance of a thunderstorm—don't seem to bother them. Most passengers seem to automatically equate all flying with whatever experiences they have had on the airlines where banks are barely noticeable .

Preflight Preparation

A certain amount of preflight preparation can help a great deal. Try to do all the routing preflighting before the passengers arrive at the airport. It tends to be disconcerting to them to see pilots shaking the rudder, elevators and flaps as if there might be a chance that they'll fall off. When they do arrive at the airport, give first-time lightplane passengers a little speech. Explain in advance about the need to bank in order to make turns. Note that turbulence, though maybe not particularly comfortable, is nothing to

Fig. 12-1. Most company aircraft are used most of the time to ferry non-pilot passengers.

worry about. Unless you're planning on using earphones, explain that it takes a certain amount of practice to understand what is being said over the radio and not to worry about it. Tell them approximately how long the flight is going to take. Preferably add a little to the expected time en route so that they don't start getting upset when headwinds cause you to be late in arriving at your destination. Make sure that everybody takes a quick trip to the john before boarding the airplane.

Once in the air, especially during the early portion of the flight, keep banks to 10 or 15 degrees. Try to find an altitude at which the air is smooth. Keep the cabin well ventilated, even if it's a bit on the cool side. You might consider using the lowest possible rpm setting to reduce the unavoidable cabin noise to a minimum. Make all control movements with deliberate slowness because nothing is more disconcerting to the uninitiated than erratic actions by the pilot and the plane's resulting erratic reactions.

As soon as cruise had been established it is usually a good idea, especially if the airplane is on the autopilot, to engage the passengers in a conversation. Point out landmarks on the ground or otherwise take their minds off the fact that they are sitting up there in that little airplane, completely helpless.

For heaven's sakes, don't accidentally run a tank dry. There is nothing more likely to induce momentary heart failure than the sudden silence when the engine starts to suck air from an empty tank. We must be aware that most non-pilots, no matter what we tell them to the contrary, are convinced that if the engine quite the thing is going to plummet to earth like the proverbial brick.

131

Have Food, Will Travel

If it's a long flight, say, three hours or more, it might be a good idea to have some food on board. People will not necessarily get hungry during so short a time. It's simply that there is nothing to do, and munching on something helps to make the time pass faster. At most bigger airports the FBOs that deal primarily with corporate aircraft will be equipped to provide a selection of tasty snacks, attractively and practically packaged for use on an airplane. But, except in pressurized equipment, it is usually not a good idea to serve booze. Altitude increases the effect of alcohol on the human body and you wouldn't want to arrive at your destination with a bunch of staggering drunks.

Keep Charts Handy

Always have the charts which you may have to use readily available and, preferably, have all frequencies which may come into play written down on a separate note pad. If the weather starts to play tricks and you find that you may have to divert from your original course or have to consider landing at an alternate, it is extremely disconcerting to watch a pilot try to read a frequency on his chart under lousy light conditions. It's also tough to see him scramble around in his Jeppesen case for a chart which he seems unable to find.

Eliminate Passenger Fears

For most non-pilots (for pilots, too), being a passenger is a terribly boring experience, always laced with that unavoidable degree of fear. The more we can do to make the time pass and to make the whole thing appear as something routine, the happier and more content our passengers will be.

One last thought. It is unwise to plan an non-stop flight which will take more than three hours. For some reason that seems to be more or less the limit of endurance for non-pilot passengers. If getting to where we want to go is going to take longer than that, it is usually a good idea to land somewhere, have a cup of coffee, walk around a bit, and then take off again.

Chapter 13

The Helicopter in Business Aviation

During the third week in September of 1979, as a publicity stunt during the convention of the National Business Aircraft Association, a Sikorsky helicopter, called *Spirit*, raced a Rockwell International *Sabreliner* from Knoxville, Tennessee to Atlanta, Georgia (Figs. 13-1 and 13-2). The purpose of the race was not to determine which was the faster aircraft. That was, of course, known in advance. The Sabreliner cruises at roughly twice the speed of the Spirit.

Sabreliner Versus Spirit

The idea was for both crews and their passengers to leave the Hyatt Regency Hotel in Knoxville at the same time and to determine who would get to the Convention Center in Atlanta ahead of the other. The Sabreliner crew and the Spirit crew started off side by side, in separate limousines. The airplane group traveled to the Knoxville Airport while the helicopter crew went to a bank heliport only a few hundred feet from the hotel. To make a long story short, the Spirit won hands down. The statistics are in Table 13-1.

The reason I mention this here is that it graphically illustrates the reason why the manufacturers of the new twin-turbine executive helicopters feel that they can claim with logic that their aircraft are faster and more efficient on business trips, in the 0 to 300-nm range, than the much faster fixed-wing aircraft.

History

The helicopter was not always considered a viable means of business travel. Only in recent years, spurred largely by the introduction of the extremely reliable turboshaft engines as pow-

Fig. 13-1. The Sikorsky S-76 Spirit.

erplants, has the helicopter achieved acceptance as a means of executive transportation.

The helicopter concept, in fact, has a very long history. It is interesting to think that Leonardo da Vinci designed a helicopter centuries before the Wright Brothers built their now famous contraption and proved the viability of powered fixed-wing flight. Granted, at the time his doodling was an exercise in futility because there was no powerplant to drive the rotors. But the principle eventually proved to be a sound one.

Versatility

If it has taken an unduly long time for the helicopter to find widespread acceptance in the civilian market, there has never been any doubt about its extreme utility and great versatility. However, the reasons, to some extent, lies in fact that helicopters have

Fig. 13-2. Rockwell International Sabreliner.

Table 13-1. Statistics on Spirit and Sabreliner Race.

	Spirit	Sabreliner
Distance traveled (hotel to convention center)	132 nm	153 nm
Total esapsed time	1:10	1:59
Time airborne	:57	:37
Indicated airspeed	152 knot	310 knots
Average ground speed (all modes of travel)	113 knot	76.4 knots
Total fuel used	560 lbs	1,210 lb
Total fuel cost ($1 per gal)	$82.35	$177.94
Cost per nm	$ 0.54	$ 1.01
Number of passengers	6	6

always been expensive to buy, hard to fly, costly to operate, and, until recently, difficult to insure (Fig. 13-3). In recent years, companies have become increasingly accustomed to the huge costs involved in corporate transportation—a million for a small corpo-

Fig. 13-3. Helicopters are difficult to fly.

Fig. 13-4. With the addition of a helicopter to the fixed-wing fleet, portal-to-portal trip time is reduced considerably if the airport is some distance from company headquarters.

rate jet, $50,000 or more for sophisticated avionics packages, $30,000 or so a year for a corporate pilot. Suddenly the dollar figures related to helicopter ownership, though certainly no lower than in the past, have begun to look less forbidding. With the addition of a helicopter to the corporate fixed-wing fleet, portal-to-portal trip time can be reduced by hours (Fig. 13-4).

Today over two dozen different helicopter models are either in production or undergoing the certification process. Eight are powered by piston engines and range in price from $40,000 to over $100,000. Nine use a single turbine engine as a powerplant, with prices from $200,000 to just under $1,000,000. And then there is the more recent category, the twin-turbine helicopter, with nine models in production at costs from somewhat over $500,000 to $3,500,000 (Fig. 13-5).

Though some of the smaller piston-engine models are known to be owner-flown, helicopters, as a general rule, are flown by professional pilots. This helps to insure the kind of utilization that is necessary to justify the cost of acquisition and operation.

In the fixed-wing field the rule of thumb is that the more an airplane costs, the faster it goes. Not so with helicopters. Since the helicopter is not usually used for transportation over long distances, speed is not a major consideration. Even at 70 or 80 knots, if it takes its passengers across the choked freeways from Santa Monica to East Los Angeles, or from the East River Heliport to Westchester County or Jersey City in minutes, in terms of time saved it is well worth its cost.

Purchase Criteria

Anyone, be it individual, small company or major corporation, thinking about the acquisition of a helicopter should carefully consider all criteria influencing such a purchase decision. First, there is the obvious: size and range payload with the fuel necessary to cover the average range. But then there is maintenance. Helicopter maintenance differs from that required by fixed-wing aircraft. In fixed-wing aircraft the power train, gears, linkages and such which operate between the powerplant itself and the propeller or fan (in fanjets) are either non-existent or extremely simple. The airframe itself is a solid unit which, under normal circumstances, requires a minimum of attention. Thus, maintenance involves making sure that control linkages, are in proper operating condition. If an engine does quit, we either have a controllable glider or a somewhat unwieldy machine, propelled by asymmetric thrust but capable of limping along to the nearest airport.

Maintenance

The difference in helicopters is twofold. The airframe consists of a solid cabin suspended on rotary wings which must keep turning in order to produce sufficient lift to keep the whole contraption from plummeting to earth. Also, the power train, gears,

Fig. 13-5. One of the third generation twin-turbine helicopters, the IFR-certificated Agusta 109A.

137

Fig. 13-6. The helicopter as an aerial crane.

couplings and linkages which connect the engine to the main and tail rotor are lengthy and complicated. If any one component along that power train shows wear, or, worse yet, malfunctions, the result is likely to be extremely serious. Helicopters suffer from a certain degree of unavoidable vibration which, over the long pull,

Fig. 13-7. One of the advantages of a helicopter is its ability to operate to and from the company parking lot.

Fig. 13-8. Noise can be a problem for helicopters operating to and from inner cities or residential areas.

tends to affect the service life of all components. Helicopters, therefore, need to undergo a continuous preventive maintenance program. This program must be conducted by a mechanic who knows the particular make and model inside out and knows where to look for early signs of looseness and wear. In this area the pilot is frequently not much help. Used to a certain degree of vibration, he is likely to be unaware of slight increases in that vibration which are the usual telltale signs of beginning wear. A knowledgeable

Fig. 13-9. A different view of the Sikorsky Spirit.

Fig. 13-10. The executive transport Bell 222.

mechanic, on the other hand, knows where to reach, what to push, pull or twist in order to determine if everything is as tight as it should be.

Before signing on the dotted line for the purchase of a particular type of helicopter, one should ascertain the availability of a mechanic. He should be located within a reasonable distance of home base, know the machine, and be willing to take care of it on a regular basis. Parts availability should also be checked. If something needs replacing, how long is it going to take to get the part which malfunctioned?

Hovering Figures

Other considerations, different from those involved in making selections in the fixed-wing field, are the HIGE/HOGE figures

Fig. 13-11. A helicopter provides quick transportation from the office to the airport or factory.

(hovering in ground effect/hovering out of ground effect). If the aircraft is to be used strictly for transportation of passengers, the hovering capability may not be of great consequence. If, on the other hand, the projected utilization includes the use of the aircraft as an aerial crane a camera platform or a means of performing geological studies, then the hovering ceiling may be of primary importance (Fig. 13-6). If all projected operations are going to take place in flat, lowland country, a few thousand feet msl will probably be ample. If, by contrast, the planned operations are in the mountains or other high country, the hovering figures must be considerably higher. Always remember that the figures given by the manufacturers assume standard temperature days. Hot summer day density-altitude effects will negatively effect these figures.

The ability to operate from the company parking lot or office building roof is a tempting one, especially in areas where surface travel is becoming an ever increasing problem (Fig. 13-7). But helicopters are relatively noisy. Before spending any money, make sure that the neighbors at your planned takeoff and landing sites won't object. Most residential communities have rules against helicopter operations for other than emergency purposes. Quite a few big cities won't let the roofs of buildings be used a heliports (Fig. 13-8). Still, the helicopter is an incredibility useful tool and deserves serious consideration by those individuals and companies which have need for its unique capabilities.

Executive Twin-Turbine Helicopters

The recent introduction of the executive twin-turbine helicopter, especially the Sikorsky Spirit (S-76) and the Bell 222, has changed the way in which people think about helicopter use (Figs. 13-9 and 13-10). As far as passenger transportation is concerned, the helicopter used to be thought of strictly as a convenient and quick way to get from a heliport close to the office or factory to the airport where a fixed-wing aircraft would be waiting (Fig. 13-11). It is now seriously considered as a meaningful competition to turboprops and even jets on missions of up to 300 nm. These new aircraft are luxurious, quiet, comfortable and, with their twin turbines, as safe as any fixed-wing airplane. The helicopter, then, is becoming an increasingly important member in the family of business and corporate aircraft.

Chapter 14
Turboprops

Turboprop aircraft, also known as *propjets*, are turbine-powered airplanes in which the turbine, instead of producing thrust as it does in the pure jets, drives a propeller. Before analyzing the place of the turboprop within the business and corporate fleet, let's take a quick look at its history.

History

It is hard to remember that less than 20 years ago there were no JetStars, Learjets, Sabreliners or Citations. The only jet sound in the corporate and business aircraft fleet emanated from the Gulfstream I which, even then before the impact of the recent inflation, cost close to a million, equipped. With the advent of the business jet, pioneered by the late Bill Lear, Grumman dropped the Gulfstream I in favor of the Gulfstream II. Most people in the aviation industry forecast that the turboprops were a vanishing breed.

But it seems that at Beech Aircraft no one was listening. The first King Air progressed from its predecessor, the venerable Queen Air via drawing boards, mockups, and the initial experimental hardware toward the family of corporate aircraft we know today. For several years the King Air then reigned in lonely splendor in its chosen field while the industry as a whole grabbed hold of Bill Lear's coattails and tried to jump onto the pure jet bandwagon (Fig. 14-1).

Then two mavericks decided to challenge the unopposed position of the King Air, Swearingen and Mitsubishi. The two couldn't have been more different. Swearingen, a designer and engineer of considerable experience and stature, was known

Fig. 14-1. Beech King Air E90 arriving at a business destination.

primarily for producing conversions of existing airframes. His initial entry was the Merlin. Mitsubishi, on the other hand, is one of the world's largest conglomoerates, headquartered in Japan, with unlimited funds to develop and market a product. Believing firmly that its MU-2 was the right aircraft to fill a distinct void in the United States corporate aircraft fleet, it embarked with patience and perseverance on the rocky road of selling an odd-looking unconventional aircraft of Japanese origin to the basically conservative American corporate buyer (Fig. 14-2).

Today the corporate turboprop fleet includes 18 different models, all but one using two turboprop engines. The one exception is the Gulfstream-American Hustler, which is equipped with a turboprop in front and a pure jet in the tail. There are six King Air models from Beech, two from Mitsubishi, three from Swearingen, three from Piper, two from Rockwell and one from Cessna. They range in price from $540,000 (in 1979 American dollars) to $1,275,000. Despite the greater speed and more glamorous aura of their pure-jet counterparts, the turboprops are now firmly established as efficient corporate transportation machines.

Craft Comparisons

Some comparison between the two types of turbine-powered aircraft may be called for. Fully equipped with all appropriate

Table 14-1. Turboprop Aircraft: Comparison Chart #1.

Manufacturer	Piper	Beech	Piper	Rockwell	Gulfstream American	Rockwell	Average
MODEL	Cheyenne I	King Air C90	Cheyenne II	Executive II	Hustler 500	Executive I	
ENGINES	PW/PT6A-11 (2)	PW/PT6A-21 (2)	PW/PT6A-28 (2)	GA/TPE 331-5-251	PW/PT6A-41/ JT15D-1	GA/TPE 331-5-251	
shp (each)	500 (flat rated)	550 (flat rated)	620 (flat rated)	718 (flat rated)	850/2,200* (flat rated)	718 (flat rated)	*pounds of thrust
TBO (hours)NA	3,500	NA	NA	2,500/3,000	NA		
SEAT crew + passengers	2 + 6	2 + 4-8	2 + 6	2 + 6	2 + 5	2 + 6	
TAKEOFF ground roll (ft)	1,712	1,629	1,410	1,458	1,370	1,458	1,506
50' obstacle (ft)	2,541	2,261	1,980	2,259	1,630	2,259	2,155
RATE OF CLIMB all engines (fpm)	1,750	1,955	2,800	2,821	3,650	2,821	2,633
one engine (fpm)	413	539	660	878	1,400/1,450	878	888
Vxse (knots)	NA	100	104	109	125/165	109	
Vyse (knots)	NA	107	117	115	145/170	115	
Vmca (knots)	NA	90	96	86	75	86	
ACCELERATE-STOP DISTANCE (ft)	3,300	3,498	3,300	3,450	3,000	3,450	3,333
SERVICE CEILING all engines (ft)	28,200	28,100	31,600	32,800	41,000	32,800	32,417
one engine (ft)	12,500	15,050	14,600	19,600	23,000/31,000	19,600	19,336
MAX SPEED (knots)	249 (12,000 ft)	222 (12,000 ft)	283 (11,000 ft)	284 (17,500 ft)	400 (25,000 ft)	284 (17,500 ft)	287
BEST CRUISE SPEED (knots)	249 (12,000 ft)	222 (12,000 ft)	283 (11,000 ft)	283 (20,000 ft)	350 (40,000 ft)	283 (20,000 ft)	278
LONG-RANGE CRUISE SPEED (knots)	236 (25,000 ft)	191 (21,000 ft)	250	250.3 (31,000 ft)	260	250.3 (31,000 ft)	240
RANGE w. res. best speed (nm)	940 (12,000 ft)	957 (12,000 ft)	900 (12,000 ft)	1,036 (18,000 ft)	2,000	1,036 (18,000 ft)	1,145

	1,260 (25,000 ft)	1,281 (21,000 ft)	1,510 (29,000 ft)	1,467 (31,000 ft)	2,500	1,467 (31,000 ft)	1,581
long-range speed (nm)							
FUEL FLOW per eng, best speed (pph)	NA	257	NA	294	510 (both engines)	294	271
economy (pph)	NA	162.9	NA	178	240 (front eng.)	178	190
STALL clean (knots)	84	89	86	82	100	82	87
dirty (knots)	72	76	75	77	85	77	77
LANDING ground roll (ft)	1,695 (1,193 prop rev)	1,075	1,430 (995 prop rev)	1,613	930	1,613	1,393
50' obstacle (ft)	2,548 (2,131 prop rev)	2,010	2,480 (1,860 prop rev)	2,100	1,500	2,100	2,123
RAMP WEIGHT (lbs)	8,750	9,705	9,050	10,375	9,580	10,375	
ZERO FUEL WEIGHT (lbs)	7,200	NA	7,200	8,750	7,176	8,750	
TAKEOFF WEIGHT (lbs)	8,700	9,650	9,000	10,325	9,500	10,325	
LANDING WEIGHT (lbs)	8,700	9,168	9,000	9,675	9,025	9,675	
USEFUL LOAD (lbs)	3,850	3,933	4,074	4,180	4,572	3,642	4,042
FUEL CAPACITY (lbs)	2,010	2,572.8	2,559.4	2,573	3,236	2,573	
MAX PAYLOAD (lbs)	1,330	2,427	1,255	2,555	2,168	2,017	1,959
PAYLOAD w. full fuel (lbs)	1,330	960	1,115	1,574	1,336	1,625	1,323
FUEL w. max payload (lbs)	2,010	1,106	2,449	1,625	2,404	2,573	2,028
WING LOADING (lbs per sq ft)	38	32.8	39.3	38.82	49.8	38.82	
WING AREA (sq ft)	229	293.94	229	266	190.8	266	
LENGTH/HEIGHT/SPAN external (ft)	34.67/12.75/40.67	35.5/14.24/50.25	34.67/12.75/42.68	44.35/14.95/46.67	41.25/13.2/34.4	44.35/14.95/46.67	
LENGTH/HEIGHT/WIDTH cabin (ft)	8.42/4.29/4.17	12.67/4.75/4.5	8.42/4.29/4.17	14.25/4.47/4.02	18.33/4.17/4	14.25/4.47/4.02	
PRESSURIZATION (psi)	5.5	4.6	5.5	5.2	8	5.2	5.7
PRICE as delivered (1979 $s)	540,280	630,500	635,890	699,500	765,000	769,000/779,000	688,453

avionics and systems, the turboprops range in price from $675,000 to $1,500,000. The price range of the pure jets goes from $1,500,000 all the way up to over $7,500.000. Still, when such big figures are geing kicked around, the initial expense involved in acquisition is never as important as is the cost of subsequent operation. Among the more popular models in both categories, the average fuel flow at best-range speeds amounts to 525 pph (pounds per hour) for the turboprops (or 262.5 pph per engine). This compares with 1,428 pph or 714 pph per engine for the jets. We have excluded the three-engine Falcon 50 in this calculation.

In the good old days, when kerosene sold for 35 cents a gallon, fuel consumption was not considered a major factor. That has changed drastically. Today that same kerosene sells for around $1.10 a gallon and has become an important item in cost evaluation. For example, assuming 500 hours of utilization per year, the average turboprop will cover 129,000 nautical miles, burning 262,500 pounds of fuel at an average cost of 16.4 cents per pound for a total fuel cost of $43,050 or 33.4 cents per mile. The average pure jet will cover 202,250 nautical miles, using 714,000 pounds of fuel, costing $117,096, or 57.9 cents per mile. Over the 10-year life of such an aircraft the average pure jet will consume $740,460 worth of more fuel than the turboprop while, admittedly, covering a 63.8-percent greater distance.

On the other hand, using one million miles for both types of aircraft, the turboprop will burn $334,000 worth of fuel while the pure jet uses $579,000 worth, though it will take a lesser number of hours to do so. To this must be added the higher cost of the major overhaul or pure-jet engines and, in all cases except the Cessna

Fig. 14-2. The Mitsubishi MU-2 is an odd looking unconventional aircraft.

Fig. 14-3. Beech King Air C90.

Citation I SP, the two-pilot requirement for pure jets. Figuring salary, subsistence, lodging and other incidentals while away from home base adds approximately $40,000 a year to the operating cost. (Actually, this may not be a major factor as most operators of turboprops use two pilots despite the fact that they can legally be flown by one).

But such pure dollars and cents comparisons are rarely the determining factor when corporations are faced with making an aircraft purchase decision. Considerations such as range, payload, and minimum field lengths plus, of course, speed, must be related to the average trip profile envisioned by the company. Corporate aircraft are primarily business machines that must be able to do their intended job efficiently, reliably and economically in order to justify their existence. The versatility of the turboprop, with its ability to operate relatively economically over short as well as long distances and get into and out of fairly short fields with ease, is one of the primary reasons for the continued growth of its popularity.

In Table 14-1 through 14-3 we have presented comparison charts, showing the more important performance parameters, describing how they stack up against one another and giving averages. Included in the charts are figures on aircrafts from Beech, Cessna and other corporations.

Beech Models

Being the pioneer in the turboprop field, Beech offers a greater variety of models than does any other company. Ranging from the economical King Air C90 (first introduced as model 90 in 1965) to the T-tailed Super King Air 200, the variety of performance

Fig. 14-4. Beech King Air E90.

specifications is adequate to satisfy most normal needs (Fig. 14-3 through 14-5). Originally all Beech King Airs were powered by Pratt and Whitney or United Aircraft of Canada engines. But in recent years, primarily because of their greater fuel economy and reduced noise levels, several models have been equipped with the TPE331 turboshaft engines from Garrett AiResearch.

Cessna Models

For a long time Cessna was the only major U.S. aircraft company with no turboprop in its lineup. Cessna used to say that it designed its Citation to combine the best features of turboprops

Fig. 14-5. Beech Super King Air 200.

Fig. 14-6. Cessna Conquest.

and pure jets. As part of justifying this claim, the company spent much time and effort in trying to convince the FAA that the Citation should be certificated for single-pilot operation. There was considerable logic in this reasoning as the Citation is as easy if not easier to handle than most turboprops, and even some more sophisticated piston twins. After much hemming and hawing, the FAA finally saw the light and did certificate the Citation I for single-pilot operation. But the turboprop market continued to look promising, and so Cessna developed the 441 Conquest (Fig. 14-6).

The Hustler

This company was formed when American Jet Industries purchased the general aviation manufacturing portion of the Grumman Corporation. Its contribution to the turboprop field is the *Hustler*, a revolutionary and unique design in which the aircraft is equipped with a turboprop engine in the front, driving a propeller, and an auxiliary jet engine in the tail. At this writing the aircraft is still in the process of going through the certification routine, but most performance parameters have been pretty well nailed down.

LearAvia Model

LearAvia is in the process of building the prototype for the *Learfan*, the last aircraft to be designed by Bill Lear shortly before his death. It, too, is a highly revolutionary design with two turboprop engines embedded in the rear of the fuselage, driving a single propeller. Since specifications for this aircraft are all preliminary and no production decision has, as yet, been reached, we have not included this aircraft among those used to figure the averages in the

Table 14-2. Turboprop Aircraft: Comparison Chart #2.

Manufacturer	Beech	Beech	Beech	Mitsubishi	Cessna	Average
MODEL	King Air E90	King Air A100	King Air B100	Solitaire	Conquest	
ENGINES	PW/PT6A-28	PW/PT6A-28	GA/TPE 331-6-252B	GA/TPE31-10-501M	GA/TPE 331-8-401S	
shp (each)	550 (flat rated)	680 (flat rated)	715 (flat rated)	727 (flat rated)	635.5 (flat rated)	
TBO (hours)	NA	2,500	3,000	3,000	3,000	
SEATS crew + passengers	2 + 4-8	2 + 6-13	2 + 6-13	2 + 6-7	2 + 7-9	
TAKEOFF ground run (ft)	1,553	1,855	1,755	1,550	1,785	1,700
50' obstacle (ft)	2,024	2,681	2,694	1,800	2,465	2,333
RATE OF CLIMB all engines (fpm)	1,870	1,963	1,755	2,850	2,435	2,175
one engine (fpm)	470	452	501	770	715	582
Vxse (knots)	99	113	111	145	110	
Vyse (knots)	110	119	125	150	120	
Vmca (knots)	86	85	85	93	92	
ACCELERATE-STOP DISTANCE (ft)	3,736	4,275	3,923	2,750	3,750	3,687
SERVICE CEILING all engines (ft)	27,620	24,850	29,100	35,500	37,000	30,814
one engine (ft)	14,390	9,300	12,120	20,300	21,380	15,498
MAX SPEED (knots)	249 (12,000 ft)	248 (10,000 ft)	268 (12,000 ft)	321 (20,000 ft)	295 (16,000 ft)	276
BEST CRUISE SPEED (knots)	249 (12,000 ft)	248 (10,000 ft)	265 (12,000 ft)	313 (20,000 ft)	293 (24,000 ft)	274
LONG-RANGE CRUISE SPEED (knots)	197 (21,000 ft)	207 (21,000 ft)	241 (21,000 ft)	302 (31,000 ft)	257 (33,000 ft)	241
RANGE w. res. best speed (nm)	1,004 (12,000 ft)	900 (10,000 ft)	1,015 (12,000 ft)	1,160 (20,000 ft)	2,070 (33,000 ft)	1,230

	1,625 (21,000 ft)	1,340 (21,000 ft)	1,340 (21,000 ft)	1,600 (31,000 ft)	2,196 (33,000 ft)	1,617
long-range speed (nm)	1,625 (21,000 ft)	1,340 (21,000 ft)	1,340 (21,000 ft)	1,600 (31,000 ft)	2,196 (33,000 ft)	1,617
FUEL FLOW per eng. best speed (pph)	354	378	335	610	215.9	379
economy (pph)	172	204.5	235	388	184	237
STALL clean (knots)	86	89	93	97	90	91
dirty (knots)	77	75	83	73	76	77
LANDING ground roll (ft)	1,030	1,390	1,290	960	1,095	1,153
50' obstacle (ft)	2,110	2,109	2,679	1,600	1,875	2,075
RAMP WEIGHT (lbs)	10,160	11,568	11,875	10,520	9,925	
ZERO FUEL WEIGHT (lbs)	NA	9,600	9,600	9,700	8,100	
TAKEOFF WEIGHT (lbs)	10,100	11,500	11,800	10,470	9,850	
LANDING WEIGHT (lbs)	9,700	11,210	11,210	9,955	9,360	
USEFUL LOAD (lbs)	4,108	4,771	4,774	3,510	4,336	4,300
FUEL CAPACITY (lbs)	3,175.8	3,149	3,149	2,700	3,182.5	
MAX PAYLOAD (lbs)	2,286	2,055	1,751	2,945	3,370	2,481
PAYLOAD w. full fuel (lbs)	532	1,222	1,225	810	953.5	949
FUEL w. max payload (lbs)	1,422	2,316	2,623	820	966	1,629
WING LOADING (lbs per sq ft)	34.4	40.8	42.4	59	38.8	
WING AREA (sq ft)	293.94	279.7	279.7	178	253.6	
LENGTH/HEIGHT/SPAN external (ft)	35.5/14.24/50.25	39.95/15.35/45.85	39.95/15.35/45.85	33.25/12.95/39.22	39.2/13.14/49.33	
LENGTH/HEIGHT/WIDTH cabin (ft)	12.67/4.75/4.5	16.67/4.75/4.5	16.67/4.75/4.5	13.4/4.26/4.95	18.75/4.25/4.63	
PRESSURIZATION (psi)	4.6	4.6	4.6	6	6.3	5.2
PRICE as delivered (1979 $s)	820,750	907,500	935,000	980,000	995,000	927,650

Fig. 14-7. Mitsubishi Solitaire.

first part of this chapter. But, since the aircraft has created a great deal of interest, we have included it in the comparison chart.

Mitsubishi Models

The latest growth versions of the MU-2 have been renamed the *Marquise* and the *Solitaire*. Both are among the fastest aircraft in the fleet. With their full-span flaps, their short and rough-field capability is one of the major sales strengths (Fig. 14-7 and 14-8). After a slow start, aggravated by a then lingering resistance to the Japanese origin and unconventional configuration (high wings, spoilers instead of ailerons) the planes today are unqualified successes. While the major airframe components are still manufactured by Mitsubishi Heavy Industries in Japan and then shipped to the United States for assembly, all systems, avionics and instrumentation are American made.

Piper Models

The *Cheyenne*, an outgrowth of the *Navajo*, is the cheapest (or, rather, least expensive) of the group (Fig. 14-9). After an extended gestation period, long delayed when the prototype was inundated by the famous flood that covered the better part of Lock

Fig. 14-8. Mistubishi Marquise.

Fig. 14-9. Piper Cheyenne II.

Haven valley and the airport, the aircraft finally made its debut in 1973. Since then it has developed into a family of three versions, the Cheyenne I, II and III, all of which are selling successfully.

Rockwell International Models

What started off as the Commander 690, a turboprop version of the piston-engined Commander 685, has now been renamed the *Executive I* and *II* (Fig. 14-10). Both aircraft have retained the familiar Commander profile which was originated by Ted Smith in

Fig. 14-10. Rockwell Commanders 840 (top) and 980 (bottom), the latest growth version of the turboprop Commander family.

Table 14-3. Turboprop Aircraft: Comparison Chart #3.

Manufacturer	Beech	Mitsubishi	Learavia	Swearingen	Swearingen	Swearingen	Average
MODEL	Super King Air 200	Marquise	Learfan 2100	Merlin IIIB	Merlin IVA	Metro II	
ENGINES	PW/PT6A-41 (2)	GA/TPE 331-10-501M (2)	PW/PT6B-35F (2)	GA/TPE 331-1OU-501G	GA/TPE 331-3U-304G	GA/TPE 331-3UW-304G	
shp (each)	850 (flat rated)	778 (flat rated)	650 (flat rated)	900	840	840(dry) 940(wet)	
TBO (hours)	2,500	3,000	NA	3,000	3,000	3,000 (6,000 commuter)	
SEATS crew + passengers	2 + 6-13	2 + 7-9	1 + 7-9	2 + 6-9	2 + 10-13	2 + 20	
TAKEOFF ground run (ft)	1,856	1,825	NA	NA	1,600	1,950 (1,350 short fld)	1,808
50' obstacle (ft)	2,579	2,170	1,900	3,219	2,620 (2,050 short fld)	2,620 (2,050 short fld)	2,518
RATE OF CLIMB all engines (fpm)	2,450	2,850	4,350	2,782	2,400	2,400	2,872
one engine (fpm)	740	675	2,210	723	650	650	941
Vxse (knots) (IAS)	115	145	NA	119	126	126	
Vyse (knots) (IAS)	121	152	NA	138	133	133	
Vmca (knots) (IAS)	86	99	NA	107	91	91	
ACCELERATE-STOP DISTANCE (ft)	3,364	3,300	NA	NA	3,450	4,075	3,547
SERVICE CEILING all engines (ft)	31,000	33,000	41,000	31,400	26,600	27,000	31,667
one engine (ft)	19,150	18,200	33,000	16,500	14,700	14,700	19,375
MAX SPEED (knots)	289 (18,000 ft)	308 (16,000 ft)	360 (19,000 ft)	309 (12,000 ft)	269 (16,000 ft)	255 (19,000 ft)	298
BEST CRUISE SPEED (knots)	285 (18,000 ft)	295 (20,000 ft)	358 (25,000 ft)	300 (15,000 ft)	263 (15,000 ft)	255 (10,000 ft)	293
LONG-RANGE CRUISE SPEED (knots)	232 (31,000 ft)	274 (31,000 ft)	326 (39,000 ft)	272 (29,000 ft)	244 (26,000 ft)	246 (21,000 ft)	266
RANGE w. res. best speed (nm)	1,190 (18,000 ft)	1,100 (20,000 ft)	1,630	NA	NA	NA	

long-range speed (nm)	1,887 (31,000 ft)	1,395 (31,000 ft)	2,010	2,278 (31,000 ft)	1,822 (25-28,000 ft)	2,139 (25,000 ft)	1,922
FUEL FLOW per eng. best speed (pph)	385	592	NA	370	313	349	402
economy (pph)	195	416	NA	230	212	254	261
STALL clean (knots)	99	100	NA	103	98	98	100
dirty (knots)	75	76.5	77	89	86	86	82
LANDING ground roll (ft)	1,120 w. prop rev.	1,128	NA	NA	NA	NA	NA
50' obstacle (ft)	2070 w. prop. rev.	1,880	2,000	3,227	3,550	3,550	2,713
RAMP WEIGHT (lbs)	12,590	11,625	7,250	12,600	12,600	12,600	
ZERO FUEL WEIGHT (lbs)	10,400	9,950	5,900	10,000	12,500	12,500	
TAKEOFF WEIGHT (lbs)	12,500	11,575	7,200	12,500	12,500	12,500	
LANDING WEIGHT (lbs)	12,500	11,025	6,850	11,500	12,500	12,500	
USEFUL LOAD (lbs)	5,117	3,975	3,250	4,700	4,300	4,300	4,274
FUEL CAPACITY (lbs)	3,644.8	2,700	1,700	4,342	3,712	4,342	
MAX PAYLOAD (lbs)	2,156	1,793	NA	2,000	4,100	4,300	2,870
PAYLOAD w. full fuel (lbs)	1,072	875	1,350	158	388	42	648
FUEL w. max payload (lbs)	2,961	2,182	NA	2,500	not possible	not possible	1,529
WING LOADING (lbs per sq ft)	41.3	65	NA	45	45	45	
WING AREA (sq ft)	303	178	162.9	277.5	277.5	277.5	
LENGTH/HEIGHT/SPAN external (ft)	43.75/15/54.5	39.4/13.7/39.33	39.7/NA/39.4	42.16/16.82/46.25	59.34/16.7/46.25	59.34/16.76/46.25	
LENGTH/HEIGHT/WIDTH cabin (ft)	16.67/4.75/4.5	21.5/4.26/4.95	12.83/4.67/4.83	17.4/4.75/5.17	33.1/4.75/5.17	33.1/4.5/5.17	
PRESSURIZATION (psi)	6	6	8.3	7	7	7	6.9
PRICE as delivered (1979 $s)	1,174,000	1,185,000	1,185,000	1,216,000	1,275,000	1,275,000	1,218,000

Fig. 14-11. Swearingen Merlin IIIB.

Fig. 14-22. Swearingen Merlin IVA.

Fig. 14-13. Swearingen Metro II.

Fig. 14-14. Swearingen Merlin IVA doubling as cargo carrier.

the design of the early Aero Commander, and which has found great favor in the business and corporate aircraft market place.

Swearingen Models

Now a wholly owned Fairchild Industries, Swearingen produces three of the aircraft listed. The two *Merlins*, the IIIB and IVA, are roomy executive aircraft with huge fuel capacities, permitting fuel-versus-payload trade offs resulting in exceptional versatility (Figs. 14-11 and 14-12). The third model, the Metro II is, in fact, a variant of the Merlin (Fig. 14-13).

Versatility

Turboprops are in a class by themselves, unique in their versatility. They provide long-range executive transportation at near-jet speeds. The same aircraft, its luxurious interior temporarily removed may be used to carry machinery to a short dirt strip at a construction site (Fig. 14-14). In the frozen wastes of the high arctic or the jungles of Bolivia or other South American countries, turboprops operate as aerial trucks, busses or limousines, depending on the need of the moment. They lack, of course, the glamour and prestige factor that is associated with pure jets. For many that appears to be a small price to pay, considering the multitude of uses to which they can be put.

Chapter 15

Flying Trucks

Not too many years ago, the idea of piling anything other than people and their luggage into a light aircraft was rarely considered. The airplanes were thought of primarily as efficient people movers and, as a result, the manufacturers designed them as such. They gave little thought to the ease or lack of same with which odd-shaped packages and bulky cargo could be loaded aboard.

Cargo Transport

Now business and industry are finidng that moving inanimate objects speedily and reliably is just as important as moving executives, salesmen and technicians. The light (and not so light) airplane, having proved eminently capable of doing the latter, is being discovered as an equally efficient cargo mover (Fig. 15-1).

When this trend started, any available airplane was being drafted into service. Packages were being piled onto empty seats of two and four-place machines or, when this proved cumbersome, the seats were removed and left home (Fig. 15-2). But this, at best, was a makeshift arrangement and soon both Cessna and Piper produced boxcar-long single-engine aircraft with huge doors, running occasional advertisements that showed multitudes of boxes and crates being loaded into those new cavernous cabins.

The reason for the growing interest in the cargo-carrying capabilities of general aviation is, of course, the drastic deterioration of the postal services, coupled with unacceptable increases in rates. Also a factor is the increasingly frequent mishandling and misrouting of air freight which, unless personally brought to and picked up from the airplane, may end up gathering dust for days on some out of the way loading dock.

Fig. 15-1. A light single-engine airplane, the Cessna Stationair 7, is put into service to move freight.

Cargo Carriers

The aircraft used in cargo transport vary considerably, with only a few being designed specifically for that purpose. Others sport any number of modifications, designed and installed by users to fit their special needs, some with and others without the legal nicety of an official STC (supplementary type certificate). They include Cessna 206s 207s and Skymasters; Piper's Cherokee Six, Seneca, Aztec and Chieftain; Beech's Bonanza and Baron 58; all models of Mitsubishi's MU-2s; the Aerostar 600 and 601; Britten-Norman's Islander and Trislander; the Short Brothers Skyvan; Israel Aircraft Industries' Arava; the immense Hawker Siddeley 748; The specially designed Guppy and Superguppy; a special cargo version of the Falcon 20; and soon even cargo versions of Canadair's widebody Challenger 600. There are also helicopters, many of which are capable of moving incredible loads

Fig. 15-2. In the early days any available airplane, such as this beautifully maintained DC-3, was drafted into service as a cargo carrier.

Fig. 15-3. Fragile machinery being loaded onto a Cessna Titan.

over limited distances. Plus, there is repeated talk of using dirigibles to move cargo too immense for transport by either rail or truck.

Inanimate objects may impose requirements much different from those of human cargo. Outsize crates require outsize doors. Weight, regardless of size, determines the maximum payload capability over a given range. The length of the average mission determines speed as well as available usable fuel. If the same aircraft must serve to carry both cargo and people, convertability in terms of ease and speed is a major consideration. And, of course, the cost of purchase and operation cannot be ignored as it affects the eventual impact on profit or loss.

Big-Iron Planes

The Falcon 20, produced by Avions Marcel Dassault-Breguet in France, and the Challenger 600, produced by Canadair in Canada, both were designed originally as plush high-speed executive transports. It was Arkansas' Federal Express which decided that they could be ideally suited to its needs. Federal Express pioneered the overnight door-to-door package delivery service between cities just about anywhere in the country at reasonable rates (Fig. 15-4). It purchased some 30 of the $2.5 million 2,000-pound payload Falcon 20s and revamped them all by removing all cabin windows, installing heavy duty cargo interiors and immense double doors that would permit speedy on and off-loading odd-shaped freight. Soon, a number of the still larger Challengers will join that fleet.

Then there is Hawker Siddeley's "Happy Hawker," the 748, a huge turboprop mini-airliner, designed strictly as a utility aircraft with a quick change interior that can be converted from 44 comfortable seats to a hollow shell with reinforced cargo floor, in less than an hour, according to the manufacturer. Costing in the neightborhood of $2.5 million, it will carry up to 8,800 pounds of payload, with the range varying between 760 and 1,050 nm, depending on the necessary trade off between fuel and payload. Few have been sold in this country to date. As what's left of the fleet of DC-3s begins to eventually fall apart, there may be an increasing market for this mastadon.

While on the subject of really big airplanes, the Guppy and Super Guppy started off as DC-7s and were rebuilt by Jack Conroy into those pregnant whales, the primary purpose of which was and still is the movement of such things as the huge satellite propulsion units from coast to coast. They are not for sale, but are available on a rental or lease basis to perform jobs which cannot be handled by any other aircraft. Stil in the "big iron" category, several companies have purchased airline jets, Boeing 707s and Convair 880s, to move such items as high-quality livestock—horses, cows, pigs, chickens—for breeding purposes from country to country.

Turboprops

Among the turboprops there are the Mitsubishi MU-2s, also originally designed as executive transports, which have proved

Fig. 15-4. Federal Express purchased 30 Falcon 20 jet aircraft to move freight in its overnight door-to-door package delivery service.

eminently adaptable to cargo work. Able to operate into and out of marginal airports in the high Arctic, the Andes and other underdeveloped areas of the world, many have been stripped of their fancy interiors in order to carry mundane machinery and equipment to construction and exploration sites. Their high-wing design which puts the doors close to the ground makes them relatively easy to load and unload. Priced at under $1 million, they can carry up to 1,400 pounds of payload over distances in the 1,000-nm range.

Short Brothers and Harland, Ltd., a company located in Belfast, Northern Ireland, produces the *Skyvan*, a turboprop that makes no pretense at being anything other than a utility machine. Looking like a huge crate with wings, it may be aesthetically objectionable, but it can carry great loads over limited distances and is especially easy to load and unload. Its payload capacity is 3,600 pounds, but the range is limited to 435 nm.

Israel Aircraft Industries, which has been successfully marketing its Westwind family of business jets in this country, also produces an odd-shaped utility aircraft designed to move cargo or, in its military version, troops (Fig. 15-5). It has a circular fuselage reminiscent of a knackwurst, the end of which is hinged and opens wide. The aircraft is called *Arava*. To the best of my knowledge none have been sold in this country so far, and neither detailed specifications nor price are available.

Piston Engine Craft

Britten-Norman (Bembridge), Ltd., a company located on the Isle of Wight in England, produces two aircraft that, though basically intended as economical people movers, are pressed into cargo service with increasing frequency. Both are high-wing piston engine fixed-gear aircraft, similar in the design concept to those endlessly stretched limousines that sprout rows upon rows of doors.

In the passenger configuration the Islander, a twin-engine version, will seat 10, while the Trislander, a three-engine machine with the third engine high up on its T-tail, will carry 18. With the seats removed, the interiors of both resemble long, narrow corridors. The only drawback, from a cargo point of view, is the multitude of relatively narrow doors which limit the size of cargo that can be loaded with ease. Selling for under $200,000 and under $300,000 respectively, they offer an 1,800-pound payload in the twin version and nearly 3,300 pounds in the triple-engine configuration. With full fuel the range is 880 nm for the Islander and 680 nm for the Trislander.

Piper's Chieftain, designed primarily as a commuter airliner, can be ordered in a cargo-door version without passenger seats. It is a turbocharged piston twin in the $250,000 range with a payload capability of 1,700 pounds and a full-fuel range of just under 1,000 nm. This is another airplane that can perform dual functions, though conversion from passenger to cargo configuration and vice versa takes a few hours.

Aerostars

Ted Smith's Aerostars, now marketed by Piper, do not at first seem to fall into the category of aircraft suitable for moving anything other than people. Still, because of the great speed, respectable range and considerable operating economy, several companies have bought entire fleets of them for the transport of non-bulky freight. A perfect example is one Midwest operator whose primary business is flying checks for banks all over the states east of the Rockies. He has been operating a fleet of Aerostars for many years on a tight nightly schedule and swears that there is no other aircraft that could do the job. He has been quoted as saying that, "If it weren't for the Aerostars, I'd be out of business." Selling in the $200,000 range, the two non-pressurized models have a payload capability of just over 1,000 pound and a full-fuel range in excess of 1,000 nm.

Beech Baron

The Beech Baron 58 must be included in this group, primarily because it is available with wide double doors. Though it is usually delivered with an interior of typical Beech elegance, the seats are

Fig. 15-5. Israel Aircraft Industries' odd-shaped utility aircraft, the Arava.

Fig. 15-6. Piper's turbocharged Seneca II has a large double-door on the left side.

removable, permitting the onloading of bulky freight. The aircraft sells for $185,000 has a payload of 1,240 pounds and a full-fuel range of 1,060 nm.

Light Aircraft

Among the lighter aircraft, those priced more within the reach of even smaller companies, Piper offers five: the Aztec, Seneca II, and Seminole twins and the Cherokee Six and the Lance among the singles. The Aztec is a workhorse, capable of carrying considerable loads over respectable distances. The trouble, of course, is that loading and unloading must be accomplished through a single right side door over the wing which, depending on the weight and size of the individual pieces of freight, is a two or three-man operation. The airplane sells for $131,000 in the normally aspirated version and for $152,000 turbocharged. The payload is just under 1,000 pounds and the full-fuel range around 1,000 nm.

The Seneca II, the single engine Cherokee Six and Lance all have the same cabin, equipped with a wide rear door on the left side in addition to a front door on the right (Figs. 15-6 and 15-7). When seats are removed, this facilitates loading all manner of bulky and awkward cargo. Dollar for dollar, the three offer some of the best bargains available in this class. The turbocharged twin-engine Seneca sells for just over $100,000, has a payload of 900 pounds and a full-fuel range of 850 nm. The retractable-gear Lance costs $66,000 in the normally aspirated version and $75,000 in the turbocharged variety. The load-carrying capacity of both is in the neighborhod of 1,200 pounds with a full-fuel range of 800nm.

The fixed-gear Cherokee Six is priced at $53,000. It can carry over 1,100 pounds and its full-fuel range is just under 700 nm. The twin-engine Seminole is really not much good as a cargo carrier, unless we are talking about small, lightweight type of freight. It sells for $83,000, can carry 880 pounds, and has a full-fuel range of 750 nm.

Cessna Planes

Cessna, too, offers a number of aircraft in this general price range. The Skymaster is a push-pull piston twin which comes in a normally aspirated, turbocharged and pressurized version. The single-engine Stationair 6 and its stretched cousin, the Stationair 7, are available with and without turbocharging (Fig. 15-8). The Skymaster models sell for $110,000, $126,000 and $152,000 in the

Fig. 15-7. The Cherokee Six has the same fuselage configuration as the Seneca.

Fig. 15-8. A Cessna Skywagon 207 being loaded with freight.

three versions with maximum payloads ranging from 1,100 for the pressurized model to 1,300 pounds for the normally aspirated one. Full-fuel ranges for all three are in the 1,000-nm ballpark. The two Stationairs run from $65,000 for the noramally aspirated 6 to $80,000 for the turbocharged 7. The maximum payload is 1,400 for the normally aspirated models and 1,000 pounds less for the turbocharged ones, with full-fuel ranges running from 550 to just under 800 nm. All these Cessna airplanes have large doors on both sides of the fuselage and, built low to the ground because of the high-wing configuration, they make loading and unloading relatively easy.

Beech Bonanzas

Though rarely thought of as a cargo aircraft, Beech Bonanzas, especially older models, are in constant use by air-taxi operators with mail and similar contracts. Today they sell in the $80,000 to $100,000 range new. They can carry up to 1,000 pounds and have a full-fuel range of around 750 nm.

Cargo Moving For Profit

The cargo moving activities in general aviation are still not too widely recognized, but an ever larger number of companies as well as air-taxi and charter operators admit that the freight activity is a major factor in making the aircraft operation profitable. Many of the commerical operators will use their aircraft for passenger operations during the day and for freight at night, keeping several sets of pilot crews busy around the clock. Indications are that freight will continue to become more and more important in the coming years.

Chapter 16

Interiors

This is a subject that most pilots couldn't care less about. Pilots are concerned with the left seat. As long as the airplane handles the way it should, anything behind the left seat seems meaningless. But it isn't meaningless to those who sit back there. Considering the amount of money which some companies spend for customized interiors, it would seem of considerable importance.

The average piston airplane, most turboprops and some jets are manufactured and delivered with certain standard interiors. If the airplane is ordered new from the factory, the future owner usually has a choice of color schemes and materials, limited to selections offered by the manufacturer. On the other hand, some aircraft are regularly delivered with bare interiors, leaving it to the purchaser to select the style, colors and materials as well as the company which will install that interior. There are many companies around the country which specialize in the design and installation of customized interiors, and there is really no limit to

Fig. 16-1. Standard interior of the Cessna Skyhawk.

Fig. 16-2. Interior of the Piper Dakota.

the amount of money that can be spent on them (Figs. 16-1 through 16-5).

Beauty Aboard a 707

As an extreme example, I was invited to a press luncheon aboard a corporate 707 which had been completely refurbished by

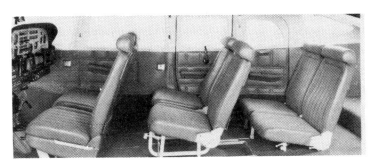

Fig. 16-3. Interior of the Cessna Stationair 6.

Fig. 16-4. Optional interior configuration in the Piper Cherokee Six, Lance, and Seneca II.

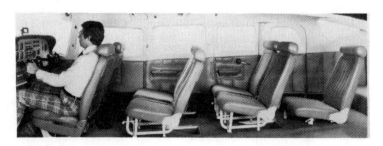

Fig. 16-5. The seven-place interior of the Cessna Stationair 7.

AiResearch in Los Angeles (and then sold for $12,000,000 by Omni Trading Floor to Diversified World Investments, an international financial organization). Starting at the tail of the aircraft and going forward, there was a beautifully executed washroom or, more correctly, a bathroom, including plush-flush toilet, bidet, stall shower, sinks and the like. Next came a bedroom with a king-sized bed, a two-place couch and a desk with a large upholstered chair, all done in silver and dark maroon velvets and silks. Forward of the bedroom was a sitting room designed for relaxing or for small conferences.

From this area one could move forward into the dining room with a U-shaped deeply upholstered couch covered in silver-grey velvet on three sides surrounding a large mahogany table. The center section was a larger area with couches, coffee tables and a wet bar, able to accommodate up to 17 passengers. Forward of it were four tables and eight double chairs, more or less airline style. Since the aircraft was equipped with an immense cargo door, this was the section where the entire left wall of the aircraft could be opened. The seats and tables here could be removed and replaced by airline style high-density seating, or the space could be used to transport bulky cargo, such as an automobile. It could be converted into a computer-equipped communications center, a display area, or anything else that the owner may one day think of. In addition there were two more lavatories, so that no one would have to wait too long, plus, of course, a well-equipped kitchen.

This is, of course, more luxury than can be crowded into the average corporate aircraft. Such items as couches, conference tables, enclosed flush toilets, a galley and a bar are virtually standard items on most of the better equipped turbo-props and jets . They can also be found in some of the cabin-class twins.

Design for Comfort

Years ago, when the late William P. Lear first introduced his original Lear Jet in a speech at an NBAA (National Business Aircraft Association) convention, objections were raised from the floor about the small size of the cabin. At that time Lear said in reply, "When you're traveling at such speed, who needs a stand-up bar, lie-down couch or sit-down toilet?" While that comment may have been valid at that time, it is no longer applicable in terms of today's corporate avaition. Many executivies spend a large portion of their working hours en route to or from distant, often international, locations. For them it is important that the time spent in the air is put to good use. That good use can be relaxing after hours or days of hectic negotiations. Or it can mean holding conferences with associates or customers to prepare for the confrontation which is about to take place at the next stop.

Designing and executing an executive interior for an airplane probably sounds a lot simpler than it is. When an interior decorator makes plans for the interior of a home or office, he or she can deal in a virtually unlimited selection of materials, fabrics, colors, items of furnishing, decoration and the like. The only limiting factors are the size and shape of the rooms involved, the taste of the customers, and the amount of money that has been allocated for the purpose.

The designer of aricraft interiors has to worry about such mundane problems as the weight of the materials to be used and the question of whether or not the interior can be made fire-proof. Everything has to be bolted down so that it doesn't start flying around in the cabin in the event of turbulence. It has to be designed to be removable, or exchangeable for high-density seating arrangements or the transport of cargo.

Anyone planning to have an custom interior installed in an aircraft, whether it is to replace the original standard interior in a used aircraft or designed for an aircraft which was delivered by the manufacturer without an interior, would be best advised to take the aircraft to an expert. Most of these specialists are listed in the World Aviation Directory. But be sure to get a firm estimate before any work is started. Prices for this kind of thing can easily go right through the roof.

Chapter 17

Making the Airplane Pay for Itself

A company-owned airplane automatically is a business machine which is expected to earn its keep. Individuals owning airplanes primarily for their personal use have a more difficult time using them in some way which would bring at least some return on the investment or permit a partial tax writeoff.

Lease-Back Arrangements

One frequently used method is the so-called lease-back. The owner makes a deal with his local FBO under which the FBO rents it out to qualified renter pilots. The details of such lease-back arrangements vary from case to case. In some instances the owner pays not only for the airplane itself, but also for all maintenance, inspections and the like. In others the FBO pays for everything except the payments on the airplane. Either way, the FBO pays the owner an appropriate percentage of the rentals which he collects for the use of the airplane.

The advantage of this type of arrangement is that the owner is not personally bothered with checking out potential renter pilots. The disadvantage is that he has to schedule the aircraft just like any other renter pilot. Unless he can do this far enough in advance, he may find that it is not available when he wants to use it.

As a general rule such lease-back arrangements work out fine if the airplane is the kind for which there is considerable demand, preferably one which the FBO doesn't have in his own fleet. Airplanes like Skyhawks, Skylanes, Piper Arrows and such are usually easy to rent because they are easy to fly. The fees charged don't have to be too astronomical. On the other hand it would be foolish to make a lease-back deal with an FBO for the use of, say, a

Skyhawk, if that FBO is a Cessna dealer and he already has a bunch of Skyhawks in his rental fleet. Quite obviously, he will rent his own airplanes first, because he makes more money with them. The lease-back airplane will just sit there to fill in when all the others are being used.

Renting the Plane

An alternate method would be for the owner himself to rent the aircraft out to others. In that case he is, of course, responsible for all expenses, maintenance, tiedown, insurance and so on. He will find that he has to spend a fair amount of time running out to the airport to check someone out, to make sure that the aircraft is properly fueled and taken care of. He, or his wife or secretary, will have to handle the scheduling, do the bookkeeping and all the attendant paperwork.

Depending on their job or profession, some owners can make legitimate business use of their airplanes. Salesmen can greatly increase their effectiveness by using an airplane instead of an automobile. Their territory extends beyond a 50-mile radius of the home town. Doctors, lawyers and other professional men can use it to attend professional meetings and conventions. If they take their wives or families along, though, only part of the trip expense becomes a legitimate business deduction. Real estate people can use it to inspect building sites from the air or to take customers to locations which are too far to easily be reached by car. Writers, painters and photographers usually manage to think up all kinds of reasons why they need an airplane to improve their work. As a matter of fact, just about everyone who personally owns an airplane tends to eventually become quite ingenious in finding ways to relate the use of the airplane to some type of business or professional need.

Foreign Travel

With more and more companies doing business in various foreign countries, it is not at all surprising that an increasing number of business and corporate aircraft find it necessary to travel beyond the borders fo the United States, not only to countries in the Western Hemisphere, but also to Europe, Africa and the Far East. No other country in the world offers the kind of freedom of the skies and all the navigation services which we take for granted in this country. Even Canada, which comes closest, is more restrictive with the reference to the use of its airspace than we are. It is, therefore, extremely important that arrangements are made in advance to obtain whatever permissions are required. Be aware of the regulations, especially the charges which might be faced, not only in the country of destination, but also those which will have to be overflown and those in which fuel stops are anticipated.

The FAA periodically publishes an International Airman's Information Manual which spells out the various government regulations, but checking its contents is by no means enough. The NBAA constantly collects data with reference to the experiences which corporate pilot have had when flying in foreign countries. An inquiry made to the NBAA may bring a great deal of valuable tips about what to do and what not to do. The AOPA (Aircraft Owners and Pilots Association), too, is deeply involved in assisting pilots with travel in foreign countries. It, too, should be contacted well in advance.

The only thing that is relatively easy to obtain with reference to foreign travel are the charts. If the AOPA is given your proposed itinerary, it will send all applicable WACs (World Aeronautical Charts) and ONCs at the same rate that it would cost if they were ordered from the appropriate government agency (plus postage). The AOPA is more efficient. Jeppesen produces radio facility charts for all parts of the world, and approach plates for all airports where instrument approaches can be expected to be made (including Moscow and Peking). A request to them, stating where you want to go and by what route, will bring all the appropriate radio facility charts with dispatch. Most of the ones covering foreign countries are printed in two colors (blue and green) and include a certain amount of topographical information, such as coast lines, in greater detail than do those published for the United States.

Planning a Foreign Flight

Always, when planning such a flight, remember that there are numerous countries with relatively unstable political situations. It would be unfortunate to plan a stop in some remote place, only to find, upon arrival, that there is or has just been a revolution, and all the rules set up by the past government are no longer in effect. Quite possibly, Americans may be somewhat less than welcome.

Don't forget to carry a lot of money. Credit cards are fine in this country, in Canada and in most of (but not all of) Europe. There are many countries, and with reference to fuel this includes Mexico, where credit cards are no good. They want cash. And with the value of the dollar tending to fluctuate from day to day, it's a good idea to know the approximate current exchange rate in order to avoid being greatly overcharged. Another reason for cash is that a few under-the-table payments to the appropriate minor officials can often help to expedite something that otherwise might take days or even weeks to resolve. It may not appeal to us, but a bit of bribery is the accepted modus operandi in a large percentage of the less developed countries. Going strictly "by the book" may cost more in time and inconvenience than a few $10 bills placed in the right palms.

Be sure to carry along an adequate supply of the right grade of oil, plus whatever minor parts may be needed to fix up something on the spot. Finding an expert mechanic with a full supply of parts in some out-of-the-way location would be tantamount to a miracle.

Planes With Transcontinental Range

With reference to trans-Atlantic travel, only three currently marketed aircraft have a truly transcontinental range. Virtually any aircraft with an IFR range of, say, 900 nm, can safely make the trip by stopping in Iceland for fuel. In addition there are a number of ferry companies which will equip your light twin or single-engine aircraft with an auxiliary fuel tank and the associated plumbing on a rental basis. The usual route for multi-engine aircraft is to fly to Newfoundland and from there past the southern tip of Greenland to Iceland. Then, after refueling, the planes go to Scotland or England or, for that matter, the Irish Republic. Northern Ireland, considering what is going on there, may not be a good idea.

If the airplane involved is a single-engine airplane, it must operate slightly differently. Canada does not permit single-engine aircraft to take off from its soil on a trip across the Atlantic. What pilots of single-engine airplanes habitually do is to go from Newfoundland to the island of St. Pierre, which is located just off the southern coast of Newfoundland and happens to be French. The French don't care how many engines you've got on your airplane. After landing there, it is perfectly legal to take off across the Atlantic.

International Civil Aviation Association

The ICAO, (International Civil Aviation Assocation) an agency of the United Nations, has been busy in recent years trying to simplify and standardize the rules and regulations affecting general aviation in its various member countries.

Everything they try to do takes forever in order to have some sort of result. It is therefore still up to the individual pilot and/or aircraft operator to make all the advance preparations necessary if one wants to fly anywhere outside the United States. But it's being done virtually on a daily basis the world over. Other countries will become aware, we hope, of the financial advantages to be gained in dealing with major American corporations. This, in turn, will make it easier for these companies to travel to and from countries in their own aircraft. Hopefully, some of the more ridiculous restrictions may eventually begin to fade away.

Photography Uses

Normally we think of airplanes as transportation machines which take us from one place to the other in a hurry. But large numbers of them are used to perform some special and often unusual functions. It is doubtful that there is any one source which would list all of these, but we thought that it might be interesting to touch on a few of them.

Clay Lacy, a former airline pilot and now owner and operator of a jet charter service, has in his fleet a Learjet which is equipped unlike any other in the world. Its sole purpose is to create exciting photographs of high performance aircraft in flight. Since taking pictures out of windows or other available openings can never be made to show another aircraft coming right at the camera, not to mention a variety of other restrictions, this Learjet is equipped with two especially designed periscopes, one at the top and one at the bottom. Inside the aircraft are still and motion picture cameras which shoot through these periscopes.

In addition, there is a TV-type camera which sees the same image that is being photographed by the cameras using film. The TV cameras are hooked up to two monitors, one in front of the cameraman, the other in front of the pilot (always Lacy himself) in the cockpit. By watching the image on the TV monitor, Lacy can maneuver the airplane into the right position for whatever pictures the client wants to get of the subject airplane. Many of of the TV commercials for some of the major airlines were shot using this equipment. Recently it was used by Atlantic Aviation to produce an introductory film of the Israel Aircraft Industries' Westwind II.

And while on the subject of photography, Tallmantz, the California-based company employed by virtually every motion picture producer who needs any kind of aviation footage in his film, owns a converted B-25. It has a large glass area in the nose through which much of the exciting footage for the two *Cinerama* pictures, as well as the aviation scenes for *Catch 22* were photographed.

Medical and Sightseeing Uses

A Denver hospital, which serves a large area in the Rocky Mountains, uses a fleet of Piper Navajos as aerial ambulances. Many of the flights involve landing at and taking off from marginal airstrips at elevations between 7,000 and 9,000 feet, quite a feat on hot summer afternoons.

A pilot living in Santa Fe, New Mexico, owns a six-seat Helio Courier which he used to conduct so-called Southwest Safaris. He flies people on extended sightseeing flights all over the area covered by New Mexico, Utah, Colorado and Arizona. Because of the short takeoff and landing capability of the Helio, he can safely stay within 500 feet or so of the ground. His passengers get views of such places as the Grand Canyon, Monument Valley, Canyon de Chelly, the goosenecks of the San Juan River, the Indian pueblos and cliff dwellings, and many more which could not be experienced in any other way. Often the flights, some of which last several days to a week, include white-water canoeing, jeep trips into remote mountain areas, lessons on the geological and archeological history of the area and more. Being able to take only five passengers on short trips and four on longer ones, the pilot is usually booked up for months and in some instances years in advance.

Other Airplane Uses

Pipeline companies use single-engine aircraft to inspect pipelines for corrosion and leaks. Many utility companies do the same with reference to their long distance high-tension power lines. Fishing fleet operators use airplanes to spot schools of fish.

The border patrol uses all kinds of aircraft from Piper Super Cubs to Cessna Citations. The planes are used to spot and apprehend other aircraft which smuggle a variety of drugs from Central and South America into this country.

Practically all important race horses are being transported from track to track by aircraft. Converted airline jets are being used to ship various types of breeding stock animals, from horses and cows to pigs and chickens, all over the world. At least one company makes a healthy profit by flying tropical fish from their native habitat to aquarium wholesalers in this country, using a fair-sized turboprop for the purpose.

The Palm Springs Tramway is a cable car arrangement which goes from the desert floor up nearly two miles, vertically speaking, to a restaurant near the top of San Jacinto Mountain. It was constructed nearly exclusively by using helicopters to move construction materials and equipment to those precarious locations in the near vertical side of that huge cliff.

Airplanes are used to herd cattle and have been used, not always legally, to shoot coyotes or other predators. They help spot and fight fires. Airplanes and helicopters are used for crop dusting, spreading insecticides or planting crops.

The variety of uses to which aircraft have been and are being put is virtually limitless. Anything that anyone has been able to think of as a possible use for an airplane has certainly been tried. New uses are bound to be developed.

Chapter 18

Aircraft Feasibility Studies

Most manufacturers, distributors and other aviation companies, when contacted by a company which believes that it may have legitimate use for an airplane, will prepare so-called feasibility studies. Based on data provided by the company, the studies examine the effect of owning one or another type of airplane on the transportation needs of the company, the cash flow, taxes and so on. On the following pages are studies prepared by the Piper Aircraft Corporation and the Cessna Aircraft Company. First are travel-cost and cash-flow analyses prepared by Piper.

Travel-Cost Analysis

When you consider investing in an aircraft for business, you'll naturally want to know: how much will it save my company? That means comparing the cost of travel by current methods (commercial air, car, etc.) versus the cost of owning and operating the airplane. Some of the factors involved are the value of traveling executives' time, avoidable overnight stays, lengths of trips, and the number of people who regularly fly.

Especially when you consider the value of executive time, chances are you'll find significant after-tax savings in owning and operating a corporate aircraft. But how can you be sure? This travel-cost analysis shows you after-tax savings from owning and operating the aircraft that best meets your needs.

What Piper does is take your travel requirements and computer-simulate your trips by each of its twin-engine or single-engine models. You specify either twin or single-engine aircraft analysis. The printout you get shows all the models which meet your needs at least 85 percent of the time, along with costs and savings expressed as estimated average yearly after-tax values. Armed with this information, you can easily see how much the corporate aircraft can save compared to your current commercial air, automobile or other costs.

Much of the input information the computer needs comes from you. You are asked for some estimates based on your company's travel experience. Piper supplies capital and operating cost data for each aircraft model.

Operating costs include fuel and oil, insurance and hangar rent, and reserve and maintenance averages as determined through surveys. Average annual capital costs were computed using the Piper cash-flow analysis program, which assumes cash purchase, 48-percent corporate tax bracket, seven years depreciation, double-declining depreciation method, and sale at the end of the depreciation period for estimated market value. Even though some of these factors for your company may be different from our assumed averages, the relative comparison among the aircraft models would remain correct. For a tailored analysis of your purchase method, tax bracket, etc., you should use the Piper cash-flow analysis program in conjunction with the travel analysis.

Ordering the Analysis Program

Simply fill out the card (which is supplied by Piper) and your analysis printout will be on the way to you within 24 hours after it is received in Lock Haven. It is also possible to transmit the inputs to Piper over the phone or by Telex.

The Piper travel-cost analysis program selects the aircraft that best meets your company's needs and computes the estimated annual after-tax savings from owning and operating the aircraft. The more accurate the information you send, the more accurate the analysis. Piper needs from you your name, your preference for single or twin-engine analysis and the following information.

■ **Range Requirement**. Needed are three estimates of one-way range requirements, in statute miles, for a Piper plane. *Minimum value* is the distance of your shortest trip. *Most likely value* is the distance most frequently traveled. *Maximum range* is the distance which would never be exceeded.

■ **Passenger Requirement**. Your estimate should include the pilot. (The program automatically corrects for this and excludes the pilot). In other words, estimate the number of seats required. The *minimum* number should be at least one. The *most likely* figure is the number of people in the plane (including the pilot) most of the time. The *maximum* is the upper limit of your seating requirements.

■ **Altitude Requirement.** This means for *sustained flight.* Since it is assumed that, in the case of single-engine airplanes, the owner will usually be the pilot, the computation of the percent of time a customer's altitude requirements are met will be related to the aircraft's service ceiling. On the other hand, in the case of twin-engine planes, it is assumed that the aircraft will be used primarily with executives as passengers (and a pilot). Therefore the computation of the percent of time a customer's altitude requirements are met will be related to 12,500 feet, the altitude above which pressurized aircraft are recommended.

■ **Round Trips Per Year.** These estimates are not for the Piper plane, but rather for the way your company is *currently traveling.* First, determine the number of executives in your company who would be authorized to travel in a corporate aircraft, if it were purchased. Second, estimate the total number of trips they currently make in a year. For example, if 20 such executives currently make an average of 12 trips per year, the number of round trips to be entered would be 240 trips per year. Please furnish an upper and lower limit for this estimate, and a most likely figure.

■ **Round-Trip Travel Time.** We need an estimate of the time an individual currently spends on each round trip. Include car travel to and from the airport, minus car travel time to and from a private plane, if you had one. For example, if the corporate plane would be located five minutes from your offices and the commercial airport currently used is 30 minutes away, be sure to include the extra 25 minutes each way in your estimate. Also include waiting time at the airport, delays, flight change-overs, etc., in your time estimate for your round trips. You should provide a minimum, most likely, and maximum estimate for travel time.

■ **Value Of Executive Time.** Make three estimates of the value *per day* of the people who would use the corporate aircraft. This value should be some multiple of the daily salary. The *most likely* value is the value per day of the people who would most frequently use the plane. An executive's worth to the company might be two to two-and-a-half times his daily salary (annual salary divided by 250 working days).

■ **Estimated Percent Of Current Travel.** For those who would be authorized to use a company plane, estimate what percent of this travel is currently by—trunk commercial air (defined for our purposes as non-stop direct flights), local commercial air (several data supplied by customer

**** PIPER TRAVEL ANALYSIS REPORT ****

PREPARED FOR
A & B & C MOBILE HOMES INC.

**** CUSTOMER SUPPLIED DATA ****

	MINIMUM	MOST LIKELY	MAXIMUM	MEAN	STD DEV
1 CUSTOMER REQUIREMENTS					
2 RANGE	300.	500.	600.	483.33	50.00
3 PASSENGERS	1.	2.	4.	2.17	0.50
4 ALTITUTE	4000.	9000.	20000.	10000.00	2666.67
CURRENT TRAVEL ESTIMATES					
5 NUMBER OF TRIPS	150.0	200.	250.	200.00	16.67
6 ROUND TRIP TIME (IN HOURS)	10.	15.	20.	15.00	1.67
7 VALUE OF EXECUTIVE TIME (PER DAY)	100.	200.	300.	200.00	33.33
8 PERCENT TRAVEL BY					
TRUNK COMERCIAL AIR	40.				
LOCAL COMMERCIAL AIR	20.				
OTHER THAN COMMERCIAL AIR	40.				
9 PERCENT TRIPS REQUIRING OVER-NIGHTS. DUE TO NO PRIVATE PLANE	50.				
10 ADDITIONAL PILOT COST (IF ANY) (PER YEAR)	0.				

1 Customer supplies Minimum, Most Likely and Maximum values, and estimates of current and future travel. The mean(average) and standard deviation (measure of variation)are computed by the program.
2 Customer requirements for nonstop range capability.
3 Customer requirements for passenger capacity including pilot.
4 Customer requirements for sustained altitude capability.
5 Estimated total trips currently being made annually by all executives who would be using the Piper aircraft. (Not the number of trips made by the Piper aircraft.)
6 Estimated round trip item currently spent in travel for each executive trip.
7 Estimated value per day of executives who would use the Piper aircraft.
8 Estimated percent of travel by trunk air, local air, other (auto, rail, etc.) transportation.
9 Estimated percent of current trips in which overnightr stays could be eliminated if corporate aircraft were available.
10 Estimated annual cost of having a pilot, if needed.

Table 18-1. Piper Travel-Cost Analysis Printout, Part 1.

183

stops and change-overs), and by other means of travel (auto, rail, etc.). All three percents should add up to 100 percent.

■ **Overnights That Could Be Avoided.** Estimate the percent of current travel requiring overnight stays that could be eliminated if you had a corporate aircraft. For example, if you estimate that out of 600 current trips per year, 200 trips could have been completed without an overnight stay before your trip's last day, your estimate for this entry should be 200/600 = 33 percent.

■ **Pilot Cost.** If the purchase of the company plane would require an additional pilot, estimate the cost per year of the pilot. Enter a value of zero if your executives would be flying the plane themselves. If you would need a professional pilot only part time, try to estimate the yearly cost. Your Piper representative can help you with this as with the other estimates requested (Tables 18-1 and 18-2).

Cash-Flow Analysis

When considering the purchase of an aircraft, the initial purchase cost (or lease-contract cost) is only one of several cash flows that should influence your selection of a particular aircraft model. Expenses, such as personal property tax, interest, fuel, oil and maintenance should also be taken into consideration. You should include the tax benefits derived from ownership of the aircraft such as investment tax credit, depreciation, interest and other deductible expenses. When taking into consideration the value of your money, you will find that the total after-tax cost of owning and operating an aircraft is often less than the purchase price of the aircraft.

The significance of Piper's cash-flow analysis program is that it gives you an accurate estimate of the total after-tax cost of owning an aircraft, relative to your company's financial position. Armed with this information, you can easily analyze your ability to own and operate any Piper aircraft. The total after-tax cost of owning and operating the aircraft can be balanced against the benefits derived from ownership, such as savings in executive time through customized travel schedules which fit your company's needs.

A Tailor-Made Program

The reason Piper's cash-flow analysis is so well tailored to your individual financial position is simple. Much of the input

Travel Analysis printout

1 Piper models which meet customer requirements at least 85% of the time are printed out. If several models meet all requirements at the 100% level, only the model offering the greatest cost saving is listed.

2 Estimated annual cost of current commercial travel by executives, based on customer-supplied current travel estimates broken down as follows:

3 Estimated cost of transportation by commercial means.

4 Estimated cost of executive time spent in commercial travel.

5 Estimated cost of additional overnight stays including food, lodging and executive time loss.

6 Estimated total after-tax travel cost by current commercial means.

7 Estimated annual cost of travel by Piper aircraft, broken down as follows:

8 Estimated Piper operating cost (includes fuel and oil, maintenance and reserve, insurance and hangar rent, and pilot cost if specified by customer).

9 Estimated cost of executive time spent in Piper travel.

10 Estimated capital cost (average annual cost of ownership based on cash purchase and 7-year depreciation).

11 Estimated total Piper travel cost per year after taxes.

12 Estimated annual after-tax savings from Piper ownership.

13 Shows what percent of time a given Piper model will satisfy the customers' requirements.

**** PIPER TRAVEL ANALYSIS REPORT ****

PREPARED FOR
A & B C MOBILE HOMES INC.

1 MODEL =	LANCE	SIX 300	ARROW TC	ARCHER
2 COMMERCIAL TRAVEL COST				
3 TRAVEL COST	10846	10846	10846	10846
4 EXECUTIVE TIME COST	36270	36270	36270	36270
5 ADDITIONAL OVERNIGHT STAYS DUE TO LACK OF COMPANY PLANE	9672	9672	9672	9672
6 TOTAL (AFTER TAX)	56788	56788	56788	56788
7 PIPER TRAVEL COST	7361	7106	6946	5319
8 OPERATING COST *	14509	15496	14396	17646
	880	719	673	413
9 EXECUTIVE TIME COST				
10 CAPITAL COST				
11 TOTAL (AFTER TAX)	22749	23321	22015	23379
12 COST SAVINGS DUE TO PIPER OWNERSHIP (A/T)	34038	33467.	33409	
13 LEVEL AT WHICH CUSTOMER REQUIREMENTS ARE MET (PERCENT)				
PASSENGERS	100	100	100	100
ALTITUDE	91	91	100	86
LOAD & RANGE	100	100	100	93
PERFORMANCE DATA				
ESTIMATED HOURS PER YEAR	554	592	550	674
OPERATING COST PER HOUR(A/T) *	13.	12.	13.	8.
CAPITAL COST PER HOUR(A/T)	2	1	1	1
OPERATING COST PER MILE(A/T) *	0.08	0.08	0.08	0.06
CAPITAL COST PER MILE(A/T)	0.01	0.01	0.01	0.00
SEAT MILES PER GALLON	60	57.	53	53
* INCLUDES PILOT COST IF SPECIFIED BY CUST				

Table 18-2. Piper Travel-Cost Analysis Printout, Part 2.

information comes from you. The computer is programmed with *your* corporate federal and state income tax rates, *your* sales tax, how much downpayment *you* want to make and what depreciation method *you* prefer. Plus, there is other data which your Piper dealer will help to fill in.

The reason the output information is so useful is simple, too. Piper has already programmed the computer with operating-cost data for each aircraft. Data includes estimates of hangar rent, insurance costs (hull insurance declines with age of aircraft), fuel service and other expenses such as maintenance and reserve. The program contains these figures determined through surveys. The program also includes current estimates of expected resale values for Piper aircraft based on blue-book estimates. You can make use of Piper's estimates on any Piper model, or provide your own estimates on the cash-flow data input card.

Choosing the Right Depreciation Method

Financing and cash sales contain options for all three major depreciation methods: double declining balance, straight line and sum-of-the-years digits. By experimenting with printouts using different methods, you can quickly find the one that's best for your own financial position.

Likewise you can experiment with different printouts to determine whether to use cash, financing or a lease arrangement. To determine which method is best for you, simply compare the present value costs shown on the printout and select the lower-cost method.

Remember, though, that Piper's new cash-flow analysis is designed only to assist you and your tax counsel in determining the bottom line of ownership. It is not meant as a substitute for his knowledge of both your company and the current tax regulations.

Cash-Flow Program

Piper computes the cash-flow analysis based on your responses to the input data requested. The program assumes that, for tax purposes, the aircraft will be used 100 percent for business. Financing arrangements are assumed to be at simple interest (annual percent rate). The printout is limited to 20 years of output, i.e., a maximum of 20 years depreciation, financing and/or lease period. If a lease arrangement is selected, it is assumed to be a straight lease. The investment tax credit can go to the lessee or be retained by the lessor.

Data Input Instructions

The cash-flow analysis can be run for any new Piper model (single or twin engine). It can also be run for used Piper aircraft. The program can also be used for non-Piper aircraft for comparative purposes provided operating costs and resale value are specified.

Give the purchase price for the aircraft, not including sales tax. Price of aircraft should be given regardless of whether a purchase or lease arrangement.

Enter the amount to be paid down at the time of sale. If the purchase is a cash deal, so state.

The estimated resale value amount for which the plane can be sold. This entry may be left blank and the computer will use Piper data on estimated reslae value based on Piper's surveys and *Aircraft Digest* data. The range based on seven year ownership should be 60 to 65 percent of the purchase price.

The depreciation period is the time over which the aircraft will be depreciated for tax purposes. It is limited to a maximum of 20 years. A seven-year period is suggested to take full advantage of the 10 percent investment tax credit.

The finance period is the period over which the loan (purchase price plus sales tax minus down payment) will be paid off. The finance period can be less than or greater than the depreciation period, but is limited to a maximum of 20 years.

The salvage value is for depreciation tax purposes only. It should normally be at least 10 percent of the new list price of the aircraft. The interest rate is the loan interest rate to be paid on the portion of the purchase that is financed.

Money value is your average rate of return on your invested capital. It would normally be greater than the interest paid on borrowed money. This is sometimes called ROI. Generally 15 to 25 percent is suggested.

Enter your federal income-tax bracket percentage, normally not greater than 48 percent. The state income tax rates for each state can be obtained from Piper's manager of Business Management Services. Enter the state sales tax percentage rate. Also, enter the personal property tax rate (if applicable). This value is usually about 1.5 percent of remaining book value (original cost less accumulated depreciation).

Estimate the hours per year the aircraft is to be used. This entry is used in computing estimated yearly operating costs (fuel and oil, maintenance and reserve), which are stored as dollars-per-hour figures.

Enter the depreciation method to be used: double declining, sum-of-years digits or straight line. If the double-declining method is chosen, the program will switch to straight line in the appropriate year to maximize the tax benefits.

If the aircraft qualifies for new equipment tax credit, so indicate. Used aircraft investment tax credit to be taken should be noted. If not investment tax credit is to be taken (for example a lease deal), note this also.

The years sold may differ from tax life and finance period. (Limit is 20 years). If you expect to keep the aircraft for eight years, enter 8 in this space (Table 18-3).

Feasibility Study by Cessna

Here is an actual Business Aircraft Feasibility Study which was prepared by Cessna Aircraft Company for an actual company. We have eliminated the name of the company involved and any data which might tend to identify it.

Cessna, like the other airframe manufacturers, will prepare such a study upon request, free of charge, regardless of whether it eventually results in the actual purchase of an aircraft. To obtain such an analysis, an interested company should contact the local Cessna distributor or dealer, or write to the Transportation Analysis Department, Cessna Aircraft Company, Wichita, Kansas 67201.

Study Purpose

This study has been completed at the request of John Doe of ABC Aviation, Inc. on behalf of the XYZ Company. The conclusions and recommendations contained in the body of this report have resulted from the analysis of travel data submitted by Mr. John Smith, President, together with a completed executive interview.

The central purpose of the study is to provide management with information to aid it in the decistion-making process relating to business-aircraft acquisition. This feasability study is an analytical approach to determining:

—If the company's key personnel's existing or anticipated travel market (total airplane miles for a 12-month period) is substantial enough to realistically utilize a business aircraft.

—If the travel market has the necessary characteristics, such as adequate trip lengths, passenger load factors, and airport availability, to utilize a business aircraft.

INPUT DATA AND ASSUMPTIONS

FINANCE RATE (APR) = 10.00   MONEY VALUE RATE = 15.00
FEDERAL INCOME TAX RATE = 48.00   STATE INCOME TAX RATE = 7.000

SALES TAX = 4.00   PERSONAL PROPERTY TAX RATE = 1.50
HOURS FLOWN PER YEAR = 300.00

DEPRECIATION METHOD IS DOUBLE DECLINING

MODEL SENECA II 34
INITIAL COST IS $ 104320.00   ESTIMATED RESALE VALUE IS $ 62592.00   YEARS FINANCED ARE 7

FUEL AND OIL USED PER HOUR IS $19.360   MAINTENANCE AND RESERVE PER HOUR IS $22.46
INSURANCE AND HANGAR RENT IS $ 3560.00   SALVAGE VALUE IS $ 20000.00

DEALER O'HARA & ASSOCIATES
CUSTOMER M & M LONG HAUL TRUCKING   4.11.77

				*** FINANCING *** ESTIMATED ANNUAL CASH FLOW AND EXPENSE SUMMARY ***					
MODEL	PURCHASE PRICE	SALES TAX	DOWN PAYMENT	AMOUNT FINANCED	TIME FINANCED	MONTHLY PAYMENT		PRINCIPAL DUE	NET RESALE PAYMENT (-)
SENECA II	104320	4173	15000	80493	7	1552			40598

	*** ESTIMATED CASH FLOW ANALYSIS ***							
YEAR	0	1	2	3	4	5	6	7
ESTIMATED CASH OUTFLOW BEFORE TAX								
DOWN PAYMENT	15000							
PRINCIPAL		9713	10730	11854	13095	14466	15981	17654
INTEREST		8912	7895	6771	5530	4159	2544	971
PERSONAL PROP TAX		1162	830	593	424	303	300	300
FUEL AND OIL		5808	5805	5808	5808	5808	5808	5808
INSURANCE & HANGAR RENT		3560	3186	3093	2999	2812	2625	2438
MAINTENANCE & RESERVE		2025	2025	2025	2025	2025	2025	2025
PRINCIPAL DUE AT SALE		0	0	0	0	0	0	0
2. TAX DUE AT SALE								21994
TOTAL CASH OUTFLOW	15000	31180	30474	30144	29881	51567	29383	51191
ESTIMATED ITEMS THAT INCREASE CASH BEFORE								
TAX EFFECT								
3. DEPRECIATION		30998	22141	19815	11297	8069	173	0
4. DEDUCTABLE		21467	19744	18290	16786	37100	13402	11542
5. INVESTMENT TAX CREDIT		0	0	0	0	0	0	0
6. CASH REC AT SALE		0	0	0	0	0	0	62592
7. CASH INFLOW AFTER TAX		27093	21630	17612	14502	23326	7010	68552
TAX RATE IS 0.5164								
8. NET CASH	-15000	-4087		-12532	-15379	-28241	-2273	17362
(- IS CASH OUT)								
9. TOTAL CASH FLOW		-89095						
10. COST PER HOUR		42.43						
11. THE PRESENT VALUE COST IS	-59461							

Table 18-3. Piper Cash-Flow Analysis Printout.

189

—If the aforementioned conditions are met, the proper aircraft to allow the company maximum efficiency in meeting its travel requirement.

—The costs of this service in terms of ownership and utilization.

—If the travel market allows the business aircraft to save significant amounts of productive man-hours and overnight stays (in addition to many intangible benefits) over commercial methods of transportation.

The costs of business aircraft transportation should be split into two categories, fixed and variable, and considered separately. The variable costs (costs of use) should be compared to the direct travel costs of present travel modes. The fixed costs (cost of ownership) should be weighed against the benefits of operating a company-owned airplane. It is obvious that a detailed comparison should be made between costs and benefits before determining feasibility of an aircraft for your company.

All of the involved entities, most importantly your business, are harmed by the misuse or mismanagement of aircraft. Therefore, we have analyzed your travel needs as accurately as possible based on the data provided, and made an objective decision concerning aircraft acquisition. Very few manufacturers of any kind of business equipment, Cessna included, can guarantee with any certainty that their product will produce a precise effect on finances. Actual results, naturally, are still as much a function of management action, policies, and decisions (and many other variables) as of the product itself.

Travel Analysis

The potential for a business aircraft is generally based on its ability to make travel more productive (reducing travel time or increasing the productivity for a given amount of time). Travel analysis deals with the specifics of how you are currently handling your transportation problems. It considers the differences between the modes of travel which are available to you. Also, it evaluates your current travel mode in light of present needs nad contemporary innovations which you may not have previously considered.

There are four major areas of investigation that help to predict the likelihood that a business airplane should increase productivity: amount and nature of travel, travel dispersion, type and frequency of airline service and potential aircraft utilization. The amount and nature of travel answers two important questions. Is there enough travel to make a business aircraft feasible, and is it the kind of travel for which an aircraft is suited? Travel dispersion categorizes the trips in terms of distance, frequency and volume of passengers. This information is useful in further defining your travel patterns and determining whether these pattern are suitable for business aircraft use. Cessna studies the type and frequency of airline service in order to conceptualize the amount of time being spent traveling and the probability that a business airplane could reduce that time. The culmination of this study is to estimate the total annual utilization of a business aircraft for your company.

Many intangible benefits accompany business aircraft use. Even though such benefits are very real and important, here they are used only in a supportive role. The conclusion is based primarily on facts indicating an opportunity for significant, measurable increases in productivity.

Amount and Nature of Travel

Evaluating the possibilities for a business airplane begins by making estimates about the overall amount of travel within the organization and the potential growth of such travel. This kind of evaluation can be more a limiting factor than a justifying one. In other words, just proving the existence of a large quantity of travel is not necessarily sufficient evidence that the company should economically use an airplane, as some trips may not be suited for business aircraft use.

The amount and nature of travel is derived from your past travel records and the executive interview completed prior to the initiation of this study. Based on this information Cessna has examined the number of trips taken, the mode of transportation and volume of passengers per trip.

The XYZ Company submitted travel data covering the month of August, 1978. This month was indicated to be representative of travel throughout the year, and therefore will be used to make annual projections within the study. An analysis of the travel within this sample period reveals that 33 round trips were made to some 17 separate destinations.

Records indicate that the company's primary mode of travel is by automobile. A typical year's travel budget for this mode of travel was not given. Airline travel has also been used by the company. Costs associated with this mode of transportation were not provided. In addition, charter service has been utilized in the past.

Poor airline service to company destinations and the emergency need to travel were listed as reasons for utilizing this charter service. A normal passenger load on these charter flights was indicated to be two to three people.

Approximately 50 percent of the XYZ Comapny's travel is of a scheduled nature (20 percent scheduled one to two weeks in advance, and 30 percent scheduled two to five days in advance). Scheduled trips lend themselves well to business aircraft usage due to the flexibility of scheduling, thereby accommodating many more trips on the aircraft. The remaining 50 percent of travel, however, was listed as on-demand type travel. For on-demand or emergency type trips, the availability of an immediate fast transportation mode is an obvious necessity.

Travel Dispersion

An analysis of the geographic, time and volume dispersions of the organization's business travel is of utmost importance to the travel analyst. The object of this analysis is to examine the environment of which the company plane would become part (the distances it would cover, the schedules it would maintain, etc.). Such an examination reveals valuable information as to the efficiency with which past travel has been made and the probability of improving that efficiency.

Geographic dispersion of business destinations partially indicates whether or not a company aircraft can be effectively substituted for present travel. If present travel is primarily between large metropolitan cities with frequent and direct airline service chances for substantial savings in productive man-hours may be minimized. Volume dispersion is the number of personnel taking trips to various destinations. This indicates the relative importance of each destination. Time dispersion is the interval between trips taken by various individuals to the same destinations or destinations having close proximity. This information helps determine the potential for grouping company trips on the aircraft, which enables the aircraft to be used most efficiently. From this investigation of travel dispersion comes a clear picture of existing travel patterns, how a business aircraft could fit into these patterns, and what beneficial changes could be made with an airplane.

The XYZ Company's travel destinations are located, for the most part, within the southeastern section of the United States, including the states of Texas, Georgia, Kentucky, North Carolina, Virginia, Tennessee, Alabama and Mississippi. The most distant destination within the company's primary marketing area was about 700 miles. Airline trip data show the longest trip undertaken to be approximately 1,200 miles to El Paso, Texas.

An examination of the company's past business travel indicates that it is not of a seasonal nature. For purposes of this study, then, we shall assume travel will occur with equal frequency throughout the year.

An examination of the trips made by XYZ Company to various destinations indicates that the most frequently visited cities were Atlanta, New Orleans, and Fitzgerald, Georgia. According to the information submitted, the remaining destinations would likely be visited with equal frequency. The frequency of air travel to these and other destintions will undoubtedly increase when a company aircraft is available. Most companies have found that passenger load factors tend to grow as executives learn how to use the aircraft to their advantage.

Type and Frequency of Airline Service

The airline services are a valuable business tool. Like any other business tool, however, they are useful only in the capacity for which they were designed. More and more, that design is lending the airlines to service through large central airline hubs and less through smaller cities. Conversely, American business continues to expand, from large metropolitan areas to smaller industrial cities. If the present mode of travel is primarily scheduled airlines, the kind of airline service available to destinations largely determines the practicality of utilizing an aircraft.

Generally, there are three distinct levels of airline service: direct, indirect via connections or none. The frequency of service will further modify the direct and indirect levels. If there are both frequent and direct airline flights to a company destination, a business aircraft's only measurable advantage may be its ability to transport a group of company travelers at a savings in total direct costs. If service is infrequent and/or indirect, a company plane can significantly reduce travel time, terminal layovers and overnight stays, as well as take advantage of direct cost savings through group travel. If no airline service is available to a company destination, the alternative is usually either automobile travel or a combination of airline and rental car use. A company aircraft can generate substantial savings depending upon the proximity of the destination to one of the more than 7,000 public airports not served by scheduled airlines.

An examination of the XYZ Company's travel, as submitted, indicates that the majority of the company's travel is to cities, with airline services. A significant portion of the cities, however, (63 percent) requires making connections due to lack of direct flights. Airline service is divided into the following classes: frequent direct, 6 percent; frequent indirect, 25 percent; infrequent direct, 13 percent; infrequent indirect, 25 percent; and no airline service, 31 percent.

Potential Aircraft Utilization

The use projected for the company aircraft is an integrated function of all the elements discussed thus far. It is relevant to address both the amount of use the aircraft would receive and the ways in which it would be employed.

A business aircraft operates most efficiently under conditions as outlined in the foreword section. The extent to which these conditions exist within the organization has been considered. One purpose of this area of investigation is to suggest ways your company can use a business aircraft. Based on this and considering your total travel requirements, Cessna can depict the amount of use your aircraft would likely receive yearly.

Measuring the potential for a company-owned airplane will require some subjective analysis. Since the dates of individual trips are not known, potential grouping of such trips for estimating use of the airplane involves an approximation of an average passenger load. Based on the data supplied by the company, the average passenger load is estimated to be two people. In all probability this estimated passenger load will increase as the company finds new ways of using the aircraft to its advantage. Table 18-4 outlines potential utilization for a compnay aircraft over a one-year period. As shown by this figure, there appears to be a conservative potential for 300 round trips covering approximately 245,520 miles. Although the aircraft will be based at the company headquarters in Montgomery, it was indicated that the airplane would be used for several trips originating from the company's branch offices in New Orleans and Atlanta. These figures have been included in the potential, per XYZ Company's instructions.

The amount of utilization indicated is likely in excess of any single aircraft's capability. This is due to the large number of potential flying hours and round trips. With this type of utilization there will likely be conflicts as to the availability of the aircraft due to other busines strips, necessary maintenance, etc. For these

Table 18-4. Frequency Distribution of Trip Distances.

Table 18-4. Frequency Distribution of Trip Distances.

Distances	# trip legs	percent	cum. percent
0-100	0	0	0
101-200	108	24	24
201-300	90	20	44
301-400	72	16	60
401-500	72	16	76
501-600	36	8	84
601-700	36	8	92
701-800	0	0	92
801-900	0	0	92
901-1000	0	0	92
1001-1100	18	4	96
1101-1200	18	4	100
	450*	100	

*The 450 annualized trip legs were determined by reducing the original 600 annualized total by 25 percent (300 round trips X 2 = 600 trip legs x 75% 600 trip legs X 75% = 450 trip legs). The 450 trip legs translate into 225 round trips.

reasons, the XYZ Company may wish to consider a second aircraft at some time in the future after initial acquisition.

For purposes of this analysis, however, the annual potential has been reduced by a random 25 percent to more accurately reflect realistic figures for one aircraft. The reduction would allow for occasional maintenance, scheduling conflicts, etc. This 25-percent reduction would result in a conservative potential for 225 round tirps covering approximately 184, 140 miles annually. Depending on the speed of the aircraft selected, this translates into a potential 720 to 800 hours of utilization over some 200 flight days. Since the estimates of annual travel are of a conservative nature, utilization of the company aircraft would, in all probability, be greater than has been shown.

Equipment Selection

A choice of the proper business aircraft to purchase, of course, must logically follow a detailed and comprehensive evaluation of the company's travel requirements, current financial position, and consideration of the intangible benefits which accrue through aircraft ownership.

The choice of the aircraft that will best fulfill the company's needs should also be the result of a detailed and comprehensive evaluation of aircraft capability as compared to those needs. The rule of thumb most commonly used as a basic guideline is that the aircraft should be no more than needed to satisfy most of the company's requirements. An aircraft with substantially greater capabilities than the company needs may impact on long-term ownership.

As in many management decisions, the process of selecting suitable equipment is a matter of determining the relative importance of each of several factors, and then making a choice which best fits the resulting profile. There are normally five principal rational factors upon which to base an aircraft and equipment-selection analysis. While all these factors are important, the degree of importance of each factor rests with specific travel requirements.

■ **Trip Distances And Number Of Passengers.** This information will help to decide the size, range and payload requirements that must be met. This factor is also important in selecting necessary or desirable equipment.

■ **Uses And Users Of The Aircraft.** Expected users of the aircraft will affect the type of aircraft, seating arrangements, performance requirements and interior appointments. Special uses, such as cargo needs, will also affect the selection.

■ **Environmental Aspects Of Route And Destinations.** The need for special systems, such as pressurization or turbocharging, runway performance requirements and navigational package is often predicted by these factors.

■ **Frequency Of Trips.** This information helps qualify the relative importance of the other factors. In addition, trip frequency requirements aid in equipment decisions, such as avionics and convenience options.

■ **Financial And Performance Considerations.** In any equipment selection decision, this information provides rationale by properly balancing needs against costs. The selection process, of course, is still subjective to a certain degree. Equipment such as cabin stereo systems, interior appointments and convenience accessories remain largely a matter of personal taste. A full list of available options has been included for consideration in such a selection.

Distance and Passengers

An examination of all potential trips likely to be undertaken by the company aircraft indicates that the one-way trip distances

Table 18-5. Analysis of Potential Aircraft Utilization.

	Average passenger density	Total trips (1 month)	Total annual trips	Number one-way miles	Total miles flown
From Montgomery to:					
Atlanta, GA	2	2	24	160	7,680
New Orleans, LA	2	2	24	275	13,200
Greenville, SC	2	1	12	280	6,720
Charlotte, NC	2	1	12	330	7,920
Greensboro, NC	2	1	12	480	11,520
Sherman, TX	2	1	12	610	14,640
Huntsville, AL	2	1	12	180	4,320
Fitzgerald, GA	1	2	24	180	8,640
Dallas, TX	2	1	12	600	14,400
Houston, TX	2	1	12	550	13,200
London, KY	2	1	12	400	9,600
Richmond, VA	2	1	12	625	15,000
El Paso, TX	2	1	12	1,200	28,800
Madiosonville, KY	2	1	12	360	8,640
Jackonsville, FL	2	1	12	325	7,800
Blount, TN	2	1	12	275	6,600
From New Orleans to:					
Sherman, TX	2	1	12	475	11,400
Jackson, MS	2	1	12	180	4,320
Dallas, TX	2	1	12	450	10,800
Houston, TX	2	1	12	340	8,160
El Paso, TX	2	1	12	1,050	25,200
From Atlanta to:					
Concine, TN	2	1	12	290	6,960
		Total amount round trips =	300	Miles =	245,520*

*As this amount of potential likely exceeds any one aircraft's capabilities, we have reduced these figures by a random 25 percent to reflect trips which will likely be made by other travel modes due to scheduling conflicts, maintenance requirements, etc. This reduction results in a potential of 225 round trips and 184,140 miles or 720 to 800 hours of flying time, depending on the aircraft selected.

range from approximately 160 to 1,200 miles. Table 18-5 is a frequency distribution of these one-way distances. As shown by this distribution, 100 percent of the trip lengths could be met by an aircraft capable of traveling 1,200 miles non-stop. You will note, however, that only 8 percent of all trip legs fall within the 701 to 1,200-mile range. Therefore it would appear more realistic to give primary consideration to those trips falling within the 0 to 700-mile range. For purposes of aircraft selection, then, the company aircraft should have a non-stop range of at least 700 miles.

Based on examination of the travel data submitted, an average passenger load would be approximately two passengers. However, it is still necessary to establish what the maximum passenger density might be for an XYZ Company airplane. Based on information obtained in the executive interview, the maximum number of people who have traveled together on past business trips is four. The company does not anticipate this maximum passenger requirement to increase with the use of a business airplane. For purposes of aircraft selection, then, primary consideration will be given to aircraft with a minimum of five seats (four passengers plus pilot).

Uses and Users

The XYZ Company's airplane will be used primarily for transporting company principals, executives and other personnel to various business destinations. Other uses relate to those indicated in the section covering intangible benefits.

Information received from the company indicates that there are no pilots within the organization at this time. Based on the number of potential hours of utilization possible, it is recommended that the services of a qualified full-time pilot be considered. There was no information provided to indicate any particular health problems among potential users of the aircraft. Thus, there does not appear to be a medical need for pressurization or other special systems.

Environmental Conditions

An examination of the flight routes which, in all probability, will be used by the company during its travel indicates that en-route terrain, for the most part, is not mountainous. A flight altitude of 5,000 feet above mean sea level would be adequate to meet the minimum en-route IFR requirements for this area of the country.

Other types of terrain that will most likely be encountered involve rough, densely wooded areas (North and South Carolina, Alabama, etc.) and swampy areas (Florida and Louisiana). Additionally, flights over water may occur in the Gulf Coast area. With the amount of travel that the XYZ Company will be doing, it is probable that low ceilings and fog as well as icing conditions may occasionally be encountered by the aircraft. The information submitted indicated that a sufficient portion of XYZ Company's travel (50 percent) is of an on-demand or emergency nature. This type of travel would, in all likelihood, require some night flying. In addition, speed in reaching the destination may be important.

An analysis of the previously mentioned environmental conditions definitely indicates the need for considering a twin-engine aircraft. For purposes of this study, primary consideration will be given to multi-engine aircraft. In addition, representatives of the XYZ Company have indicated that their primary area of interest is in multi-engine aircraft.

If high altitudes en route are anticipated, or rapid climbs and descents are of concern, then the company may wish to consider a pressurized aircraft. Likewise, if high altitudes en route or landings at high elevation airports are anticipated, the company may wish to consider turbocharging. It's a mechanical system that allows full engine power to be maintained while operating in rarefied air at high altitudes.

While examination of the environmental aspects of routes and destinations does not necessarily indicate the need for pressurization or turbocharging, the company has indicated that it desires to consider only aircraft with these characteristics. This decision indicates the company's obvious concern for the comfort of the passengers. In addition—the company is no doubt, aware of the operating efficiencies of aircraft at these higher altitudes. For purposes of this study, then, consideration will be given to pressurized aircraft.

Frequency of Trips

Earlier a potential for 225 round trips was indicated, accounting for approximately 720 to 800 hours of utilization annually. Since this appears to inidcate an above average utilization rate, it is recommended that the aircraft selected have IFR capability, full de-icing equipment for all-weather capability, dual communications and navigational equipment (including copilot instrument panel) and an autopilot. The prevailing weather experienced in the

Table 18-6. Statistics on the Four Cessna Models.

Model	Seats	Service ceiling S/E	M/E	max rec. cruising speed (mph)	max range (stand. tanks)
Cessna 340 II	6	15,800'	29,800'	264	1,193sm*
Cessna 414 II	8	19,850'	31,350'	259	1,508 sm
Cessna 421 II	8	14,900'	30,200'	279	1,260 sm*
Cessna Conquest	11	21,380'	37,000'	337	2,529 sm

*Optional long-range fuel tanks available.

various parts of the country in which the company will be flying adds validity to these recommendations.

Financial and Performance Considerations

To complete the profile of a suitable airplane for XYZ Company, the cost factors should be examined against the relative merit of airplanes which can fill the travel requirements of the company. Within the criteria established, there are at least four Cessna models which appear to meet these needs. They are the Cessna 340 II, 414 II, 421 II and Conquest. See Table 18-6.

These airplanes differ in two other important respects: the extent to which they meet the load and range parameters and their prices. A comparison of price versus performance will provide a basis for a practical choice between the four.

For this analysis the four airplanes have been compared on a useful load and price basis. Useful load is the amount of weight the airplane is designed to carry over and above the empty weight of the aircraft. This load includes all people on board plus luggage and fuel. Table 18-7 shows the useful load requirements for a hypothetical 700-mile trip with two passengers and one pilot. Also see Table 18-8.

Table 18-7. Useful Load Requirements for a 700-Mile Trip.

	340II	414II	421II	Conquest
Pilots, bags & charts	210	210	210	210
Passengers - two at 170 pounds each	340	340	340	340
Fuel (pounds)	833*	850*	1,015**	1,094***
Baggage (20 pounds per pass.)	40	40	40	40
Useful load required	1,423	1,440	1,605	1,684

* cruise at 20,000 ft. 74.8% power, no wind, 100 sm+45 min res.
**cruise at 20,000 ft. 73.5% power, no wind, 100 sm+45 min. res.
***cruise at 33,000 ft. 96.0% power, no wind, 100 sm+45 min. res.

Table 18-8. Useful Load Capacity Figures.

	340 II	414 II	421 II	Conquest
Base airplane useful load	1,882	2,262	2,737	4,336
Optional equipment weight*	– 342	– 421	– 452	– 317
Useful load capacity	1,540	1,841	2,285	4,019

*Optional equipment used is typical for an average equipped aircraft.

Since it appears that all four airplanes meet the load and range parameters, a price comparison is necessary. The comparison below in Table 18-9 is based only on the manufacturer's suggested list price.

This price comparison suggests that, strictly from an economic standpoint, the Cessna 340 II should be the aircraft recommended. The remainder of the study, then, will be based on the recommendation that the XYZ Company give primary consideration to the acquisition of a Cessna 340 II.

Cost of Ownership

Having selected the appropriate airplane, it is now time to analyze the costs that are necessary to realize the benefits of its use. To do this, the costs arising from ownership of the airplane will be considered separately from those costs associated with its operation. It is recommended that your accountant's opinion be sought in the proper method of pricing the aircraft for tax and reporting purposes. However, this suggested separation allows the most realistic method of analyzing the costs versus the benefits of utilizing a company airplane. For this study, assume that the decision to use the airplane should be based on a comparison of the direct travel costs involved. Likewise, the costs of ownership of

Table 18-9. Price Comparison Figures.

Airplane	Base price	Differential as % of lower-cost aircraft
Cessna 340 II	$242.490	—
Cessna 414 II	$306,240	26%
Cessna 421 II	$369,240	52%
Conquest	$925,000	281%

Table 18-10. Fixed Costs.

ITEMS	ESTIMATED COST PER YEAR
Pilot salary (1)	$16,500
Insurance (2)	4,013
Hangar rental (3)	1,500
Annual inspection	675
Crew training (4)	520
Miscellaneous (5)	1,000
Yearly fixed costs(6)	$25,008

(1) $15,000 = 10% fringe benefits.
(2) 0 deductible, $5 million single-limit liability
    (passenger liability, public damage, medical)
(3) $125 per month.
(4) Six hours for one pilot@ $86.72 per hr. ($71.82
    direct operating costs + $15/hr check fee)
(5) Charts, subsciptions, personal property tax,
    dues, stores, etc.
(6) Does not include depreciation, interest or lease
    expense. These are itemized individually in the financial state-
    ment analysis.

that airplane should be compared to the savings in terms of man-hours, reduced number of overnight stays and resulting expenses, as well as the many intangible benefits associated with business aircraft usage.

The assumption throughout this section will be "worst case," that is, assuming no utilization at all. This amounts to the equivalent of acquiring the aircraft, hiring a crew, insuring the aircraft and then leaving it parked in a hangar. No operational savings are considered in this section. In later sections probable savings will be examined more closely. The basic analysis in this section will encompass the effects of ownership costs on the income statement and cash flow resulting from an outright purchase, a financed purchase or a true lease arrangement. For comparison purposes, current finance rates and lease provisions of the Cessna Finance Corporation have been used. The effect of taxes has been shown by slightly increasing the federal tax rates as a provision for state and local taxes. Reasonable estimates have been provided of certain ownership costs, such as hangar rental, insurance, pilot's expense, etc., as they relate to the proposed home base and area of operation. Likewise, a conservative estimate has been made of the resale price of the aircraft for disposal purposes. These compilations are for analytical purposes; a tax advisor can make specific recommendations for record keeping applications. Tables 18-10 thorugh 18-15 show the different costs of ownership (fixed costs).

Table 18-11. Financial Statement Assumptions.

1) Aircraft acquistion
   Manufacturers equipped list price $291.940
   Sales tax @ 3%   8,758
                                                              $300,698

2) Fixed costs - $25,008
3) Depreciation - double declining balance method for book
     and tax purposes. Seven-year life with 20% residual
     value assumed.
4) Income taxes - 50% includes federal, state and local taxes.
5) Financing - 20% downpayment, 6-year term, 11.50 APR.
6) Lease - true lease, 7% security deposit with primary
     6-year term with yearly extensions at 40% of original
     rate.
7) Investment tax credit - full 10% allowed.
8) Disposal price-$154,730 - This figure is based on the
     present retail price of a similar seven-year-old air-
     plane in ratio to its original selling price.
9) Reserves - a portion of direct operating costs are
     reserves for equipment overhaul. Even though we have
     assumed this expense is to be offset by airline fares
     or other alternative travel costs, it creates a positive short-term
     cash flow until the overhaul expenditure
     is actually made.
10) Mariginal approach - the following statements are pre-
     sented in a manner that shows what changes would occur
     in the company's actual statement as a result of this aquisition.

Table 18-12. Income Statement and Cash Flow (Purchase Option).

INCOME STATEMENT (PURCHASE OPTION)

	YEAR 1	YEAR 2	YEAR 3	YEAR 4	YEAR 5	YEAR 6	YEAR 7
Cost increases							
Fixed costs	$25,008	$25,008	$25,008	$25,008	$25,008	$25,008	$25,008
Depreciation	83,411	59,579	42,446	30,397	17,606	0	0
Sales tax	8,758	-	-	-	-	-	-
Gain on disposal	-	-	-	-	-	-	-96,342
Total increases	$117,177	$84.587	$67,565	$55,406	$42,614	$25,008	-$71,333
Tax reductions							
Fixed costs	$12,504	$12,504	$12,504	$12,504	$12,504	$12,504	$12,504
Depreciation	41,705	29,789	21,278	15,198	8,803	0	0
Sales tax	4,379	-	-	-	-	-	-
ITC	29,194	-	-	-	-	-	-
Gain on disposal	-	-	-	-	-	-	-$48,171
Total reductions	$87,782	$42,293	$33,782	$27,703	$21,307	$12,504	-$35,666
Change in income	-$29,394	-$42,293	-$33,782	-$27,703	-$21,307	-$12,504	+$35,666

CASH FLOW (FINANCE OPTION)

	YEAR 1	YEAR 2	YEAR 3	YEAR 4	YEAR 5	YEAR 6	YEAR 7
Additional sources							
Net income	-$29,394	-$42,293	-$33,782	-$27,703	-$21,307	-$12,504	+$35,666
Depreciation	83,411	59,579	42,556	30,397	17,606	0	0
Sale of aircraft	-	-	-	-	-	-	58,388
Total sources	$54,016	$17,285	$ 8,774	$ 2,694	-$3,700	-$12,504	+$94,054
Additional uses							
purchase	$291,940	-	-	-	-	-	-
Total uses	$291,940	-	-	-	-	-	-
Total change	-$237,923	+$17,285	+$8,774	+$2,694	-$3,700	-$12,504	+$94,054

Table 18-13. Income Statement and Cash Flow (Finance Option).

INCOME STATEMENT (FINANCE OPTION)						
Cost increases						
Fixed costs	$25.008	$25.008	$25.008	$25.008	$25.008	$25.008	$25.008
Depreciation	83.411	59.579	42.556	30.397	17.606	0	0
Sales tax	8.758						
Interest	25.377	21.898	17.998	13.624	8.720	3.222	0
Gain on disposal							-96.342
Total increases	$142.555	$106.486	$85.563	$69.030	$51.335	$28.230	-$71.333
Tax reductions						
Fixed costs	$12.504	$12.504	$12.504	$12.504	$12.504	$12.504	$12.504
Depreciation	41.705	29.789	21.278	15.198	8.803	0	0
Sales tax	4.379						
Interest	12.688	10.949	8.999	6.812	4.360	1.611	0
ITC	29.194						
Gain on disposal							$48.171
Total reductions	$100.471	$53.243	$42.781	$34.515	$25.667	$14.115	$35.666
Change in income	-$42.083	-$53.243	-$42.781	-$34.515	-$26.667	-$14.115	+$35.666

CASH FLOW (FINANCE OPTION)						
Additional sources						
Net income	-$42.083	-$53.243	-$42.782	-$34.515	-$25.667	-$14.115	+$35.666
Depreciation	83.411	59.579	42.556	30.397	17.606	0	0
Aircraft loan	233.552						
Sale of aircraft							$58.388
Total sources	$274.879	$6.336	-$224	-$4.117	-$8.061	-$14.115	+$94.054
Additional uses						
Purchase	$291.940						
Principal pmt	28.688	32.166	36.067	40.441	45.344	50.843	0
Total uses	$320.628	$32.116	$36.067	$40.441	$45.344	$50.843	
Total change	$45.748	$25.830	$36.292	$44.558	$53.406	$84.958	+$94.054

Cost of Use

In the previous section the cost of ownership (fixed costs) was outlined and its effect on the financial statements considered. It should be remembered that those figures were compiled and their effects summarized pessimistically, assuming no utilization at all. Now, in dealing with the costs of using the aircraft, no further examination of the fixed costs' effect on the financial statements need be made. The rationale applied here is that those direct costs would be approximately equal to or less than

Table 18-14. Income Statement and Cash Flow (Lease Option).

INCOME STATEMENT (LEASE OPTION)						
Cost increases						
Fixed costs	$25.008	$25.008	$25.008	$25.008	$25.008	$25.008	$25.008
Lease expense	61.132	61.132	61.132	61.132	61.132	61.132	24.452
Total increases	$86.140	$86.140	$86.140	$86.140	$86.140	$86.140	$49.461
Tax reductions						
Fixed costs	$12.504	$12.504	$12.504	$12.504	$12.504	$12.504	$12.504
Lease expense	30.566	30.566	30.566	30.566	30.566	30.566	12.226
ITC	29.194						
Total reductions	$72.246	$43.070	$43.070	$43.070	$43.070	$43.070	$24.730
Change in income	-$13.876	$43.070	$43.070	$43.070	$43.070	$43.070	$24.730

CASH FLOW (LEASE OPTION)						
Additional sources						
Net income	-$13.876	-$43.070	-$43.070	-$43.070	-$43.070	-$43.070	-$24.730
deposit							20.435
Total sources	-$13.876	-$43.070	-$43.070	-$43.070	-$43.070	-$43.070	-$24.730
Additional uses						
Deposit	$20.435						
Total uses	$20.435						
Total change	$34.312	-$43.070	-$43.070	-$43.070	-$43.070	-$43.070	-$4.294

Table 18-15. Summary of Financial Statement Effects.

	COST OF OWNERSHIP EFFECTS SUMMARY OF FINANCIAL STATEMENT EFFECTS					
	NET INCOME			CAHS FLOW		
	PURCHASE	FINANCE	LEASE	PURCHASE	FINANCE	LEASE
Year 1	-$29,394	-$42,083	-#13,876	-$237,923	-$45,748	-$34,312
Year 2	-$42,293	-$53,243	-$43,070	$ 17,285	-$25,830	-$43,070
Year 3	-$33,782	-$42,781	-$43,070	$ 8,774	-$36,292	-$43,070
Year 4	-$27,703	-$34,515	-$43,070	$ 2,694	-$44,558	-$43,070
Year 5	-$21,307	-$25,667	-$43,070	-$ 3,700	-$53,406	-$43,070
Year 6	-$12,504	-$14,115	-$43,070	-$ 12,504	-$64,958	-$43,070
Year 7	$35,666	$35,666	-$24,730	$,94,054	$94,054	-$ 4,294
Totals	-$131,319	-$176,740	-$253,958	-$131,319	-$176,740	-$253,958
7-year average	-$ 18,759	-$ 25,248	-$ 36,279	-$ 18,759	-$ 25,248	-$ 36,279

Table 18-16. Estimated Cost of Use Figures.

Estimated Cost of use

Direct operating costs	Cost/hour
Fuel (1)	$28.90
Oil (2)	.81
Routine engine maintenance (3)	10.08
Routine airframe maintenance (4)	5.92
Miscellaneous variable expense (5)	2.00
Total direct operating cost	$47.71

Reserves

Engine overhaul (6)	14.14
Propellers	1.25
Avionics (7)	4.69
Systems (8)	3.93
Total reserves	$24.01
Total cost of use per flight hour	$71.72

(1) $0.85/gal. ⁽¹⁾ 34 gph (74.8% power).
(2) $4.20/gal. X .1925 gph (includes changes)
(3) Spark plugs, filters, accessories, etc.
(4) TIres, brakes, batteries, avionics, instruments, etc.
(5) Landing and parking fees, stores etc. Does not include waiting time or overnight-stay expenses.
(6) Average of first overhaul and factory-remanufactured engine ⁽¹⁾ 1,400 hours.
(7) 10% of avionics options ⁽¹⁾ 1,000 houurs.
(8) Mechanical systems, accessories.

the costs of that same trip by other modes of travel. Thus there would be no appreciable change in the financial statements caused by usage, merely the substitution of one form of travel costs for another. This concept furthers the "worst case" position by ignoring the possibility of cost savings except in extreme cases. These savings will be identified in the next section. A detailed comparison of all travel benefits between modes will be made in the concluding section.

While travel expenses of other modes of travel are based on ticket fares or actual mileage charged, direct operating expenses for the airplane are normally accrued on the basis of flight hours. These hourly rates are conservatively based on projected home-base and area-of-operation information and are compiled in the following manner.

Direct Operating Expenses and Reserves

These are the actual expenses of fuel, oil, routine maintenance, etc., which occur as a direct result of hours flown. For instance, oil is consumed on an hourly basis and is also changed after a certain number of hours have been flown.

Certain charges for operation must be made on an hourly basis to account for expenses which will be incurred after a specific number of flight hours. Some aircraft components have predetermined or expected normal service lives which can be used to calculate an hourly cost-of-operation figure. Other reserve components are accounted for by conservative estimates of maintenance requirements, or reserves for maintenance on avionics and airframe. See Table 18-16.

As indicated, the total hourly cost-of-use figure is an estimate. Your actual total hourly cost of use may vary from the figure shown. This may be due to differences in the cost of such items as fuel and oil, labor services, engine overhaul, remanufactured engines and avionics. In addition, the manner in which the aircraft is flown and used will have a direct effect on your actual hourly cost of use (number of hours flown annually, power settings used, type of airports encountered, environmental conditions, experience of pilot, etc.).

Value Analysis

To this point the analysis has been "worst case," considering only the costs associated with business aircraft usage and disregarding any benefits. The cost may be small, or it may be so large as to make the aircraft prohibitive. A decision must be made by management, but first other elements must be added.

The problem facing the purchaser of a business aircraft is how to relate the worth of the aircraft to the aircrafts cost. This relationship between product worth and product cost is known as *product value* and is addressed in this section.

A quantitative comparison of actual business trips taken by the company is selected from the sample travel data submitted. The comparison depicts the difference in travel costs, travel time and overnight stays required between present travel modes and the business aircraft that has been recommended. In the form presented, this comparison will substantiate the relative equivalence of the airplane's direct costs versus present travel costs. It will, in addition, provide a clear indication of the level of manpower savings that are likely to result through the utilization of this airplane on these trips.

Based on these comparisons and the other sample travel data submitted, a conservative projection of years savings of man-hours

Table 18-17. Trip A Data.

TRIP A
Montgomery-Fitzgerald-Montgomery

Automobile

Trip	Status	Time	Elapsed time	Mode	Cost	RONs	Morale time
Dpt	Montgomery	4:00p			$39.90		4:00
Arr	Fitzgerald (RON)	9:00p	5:00	Auto	45.00	1	
	(Meeting 8:00a to 12:00; incl. lunch)						
Dpt	Fitzgerald	12:00					
Arr	Montgomery	5:00p	5:00	Auto	39.90		
			Totals	10 man-hours	$124.80	1	4:00
			x 2 passengers	20 man-hours	169.80	2	8:00

Cessna 340 II

Arr	Airport	8:00a	:15				
Dpt	Montgomery	8:15a	1:00	C 340	$71.72		
Arr	Fitzgerald	9:15a	:20	Taxi	4.00		
	Airport to Meeting 9:35						
	(Meeting 9:35a to 1:35p incl. lunch)						
	Meeting to Airport 1:55	:20		Taxi	4.00		
Dep	Fitzgerald	2:10	:15				
Arr	Montgomery	3:10	1:00	C 340	71.72		
			Totals	3:10 man-hours	$151.44	0	:00
			x 2 passengers	6:20 man-hours	$151.44	0	:00

Trip wrap-up

	Travel time	Travel cost	RONs	Morale time
Automobile	20:00 man-hrs	169.80	2	8:00
Cessna 340 II	6:20 man-hrs	151.44	0	:00
Savings with 340 II	13:40 man-hrs	18.36	2	8:00

207

Table 18-18. Trip B Data.

TRIP B
Montgomery-Greensboro Montgomery

Airlines

Trip	Status	Time		Elapsed time	Mode	Cost	RONs	Morale time
Arr	Airport	6:30a	CDT					1:30
Dep	Montgomery	7:00	EDT	:30	EA-580	$65.00		
Arr	Greensboro	10:30a		2:30	Limo	7.00		
Dep	Airport	10:50a		:20				
Arr	Meeting	11:20a		:30	Limo	7.00		
	Meeting 11:20 a to 3:20p - incl. lunch							
Arr	Airport	3:50p		:30	Limo	7.00		
	Dinner 5:00p to 5:45p							
Dep	Greensboro	6:08p		1:33	EA-371	50.00		
Arr	Atlanta	7:18p		1:10				
Dep	Atlanta 7:43p	8:04p	EDT	:46	EA-561	55.0		3:03
Arr	Montgomery	7:43	CDT	:39				4:33
Dep	Airport	8:03p		:20				9:06
	Totals			8:48	man-hrs	354.00	0	
	x 2 passengers			17:36	man-hrs		0	

Cessna 340 II

Trip	Status	Time		Elapsed time	Mode	Cost	RONs	Morale time
Arr	Airport	8:00a	CDT	:15	C 340	147.00		
Dep	Montgomery	8:15a	EDT	2:03	Taxi	7.00		
Arr	Greensboro	11:18a		:30				
Arr	Meeting	11:48a						
	Meeting 11:48a to 3:50p, incl lunch							
Arr	Airport	4:20p	EDT	:30	Taxi	7.00		:48
Dep	Greensboro	4:35p	CDT	:15				:48
Arr	Montgomery	5:39p		2:03	C 340	147.00		1:36
Dep	Airport	5:48p		:10				
	Totals			5:46	man-hrs	$308.00	0	
	x 2 passengers			11:32	man-hrs	308.00	0	

Trip Wrap-up

	Travel time	Travel cost	RONs	Morale time
Airlines	17:36 man-hrs	$354.00	0	9:06
Cessna 340 II	11:32 man-hrs	$308.00	0	1:36
Savings w. 340	6:04 man-hrs	$46.00	0	7:30

and overnight stays has been made. No attempt has been made to place a dollar value on these productivity and morale savings. The value of these savings, together with the accompanying intangible benefits, should, in theory, offset the average annual cost of ownership in order to justify acquisition of a company aircraft. In comparing travel times it has been assumed that the most favorable travel connections were made using the present modes, and that no delays were encountered. Performance figures for the proposed company airplane have been conservatively estimated, assuming an instrument flight plan and routing (a more time-consuming figure). This section of the analysis, then, is an attempt at continuing the "worst case" consideration of the business-owned airplane.

Ground Rules for Comparison

For purposes of this analysis, three round trips, typical of those normally taken by the company, have been chosen for comparison. Each of these trips represents a group of similar trips normally taken by XYZ Company. For example, Table 18-17 shows round trips in the 301 to 700-mile range. Trip A is representative of this group. Trips B and C represent distances of 701 to 1,000 miles and 1,001 to 1,300 miles. Other trips could have been selected, but these were considered typical and used in this analysis. See Tables 18-18 and 18-19.

The individual trips are first compared. Then a wrap-up extending these individual totals by the number of projected occurrences for the type of trip based on trip distance, airline service, and passenger load will be used to extrapolate the anticipated annual manpower savings that XYZ Company could expect to achieve. Except for Trip C, all trips and their derived totals are based on a passenger density of two people traveling to a three-hour business meeting. For Trip C we have assumed a passenger load of three and a business meeting lasting three hours. Airline schedules and fares are based on the current edition of the *Official Airline Guide.*

Time allowed for enplaning and deplaning varies from 30 minutes to one hour, depending on size of airport, baggage, etc. Aircraft direct operating costs are based on the hourly cost of use developed in the previous section, while aircraft performance is taken from the owner's manual. Time allowed for enplaning and deplaning with the business aircraft is 15 minutes. Costs associated with rental car use are based on $16 per day and 16 cents per mile. Costs associated with company automobiles have been

TRIP C
Montgomery-Sherman-Montgomery

Airlines

Trip	Status	Time	Elapsed time	Mode	Cost	RONs	Morale time
Arr	Airport	8:35a	:35				
Dep	Montgomery	9:08a CDT	:33	EA-570	$80.00		
Arr	Atlanta	10:35a EDT	:47				
Dep	Atlanta	11:55a EDT	1:20	EA-525	28.00		
Arr	Dallas	12:47p CDT	1:52				
Dep	Dallas	2:50p	1:03*	Rental car	45.00		
Arr	Sherman	4:15p	1:25		11.20	1	
	Meeting 4:15 to 5:15p						
	Stay overnight						
	Meeting 8:00a to 10:00a						
Arr	Dallas	11:25a	1:25	Rental car			
Dep	Dallas	12:20p CDT	:55				
Arr	Atlanta	3:10p EDT	1:50	EA-524			
Dep	Atlanta	3:53p EDT	:43		80.00		
Arr	Montgomery	3:36p CDT	:43	EA-661			
Dep	Airport	4:05p	:29				
	Totals		13:40 man-hrs		$244.20	—	:00
	× 3 passengers		41:00 man-hrs		$654.20	3	:00

Cessna 340 II

Trip	Status	Time	Elapsed time	Mode	Cost	RONs	Morale time
Arr	Airport	8:00a	:15				
Dep	Montgomery	8:15a	2:45	C 340	197.20		
Arr	Sherman	11:00a	:20	Taxi	3.00		
Arr	Meeting	11:20a					
	Meeting 11:20a to 3:20p. incl. lunch						
Arr	Airport	3:40p	:20	Taxi	3.00		
Dep	Sherman	3:55p	:15				
Arr	Montgomery	6:40p	2:45	C 340	197.20		
Dep	Airport	6:50p	:10				
	Totals		6:50 man-hrs		400.40	0	1:50
	× 3 passengers		20:30 man-hours		400.40	0	1:50
							5:30

Wrap-up

	Travel time	Travel cost	RONs	Morale time
Airlines	41:00 man-hrs	$654.20	3	:00
Cessna 340 II	20:30 man-hrs	$400.40	0	5:30
Saving w. 340	20:30 man-hrs	$253.80	3	(5:30)

(*excludes one hour lunch)

Table 18-19. Trip C Statistics.

210

set at 19 cents per mile. An average speed of 50 mph was assumed for this mode of travel. When necessary, trips allow one hour for meals, which is not included as travel time. Motel costs associated with overnight stays have been set at $45 per night, per person, to cover cost of room, meals and miscellaneous items.

Three types of costs are tabulated in these comparisons: dollar costs, including airline fares, airplane costs, automobile costs, and overnight expenses; elapsed-time costs, or the number of productive man-hours lost in travel; and morale costs, including both nights away from home and off-hours travel before 8:00 a.m. and after 5:00 p.m. See Table 18-20.

Company Savings

A comprehensive survey of all costs of operating and acquiring a company airplane has been completed. The value analysis section has applied those costs to a comparison of travel times and expenses between the airlines and automobile and the Cessna 340 II.

Based only on the three types of trips analyzed, it is estimated that XYZ Company could save a minimum of 3,048 man-hours and 414 unnecessary overnight stays annually. As stated previously, no attempt has been made to place a value on the man-hour savings; nor has any formula been offered to compute that value. The real value lies not only in the attendant expenses involved in overnight stays and unproductive travel time, but in morale costs as well. Morale costs or morale time is the fourth element of total savings. It includes both the off-hours travel (before 8:00 a.m. and after 5:00 p.m.) and the time spent away from home overnight. On an annualized basis it was shown that, in addition to the 414 man-overnights, at least 1,048 man-hours of employees' personal time would be saved. To achieve these savings, the company could expect average increases in the out-of-pocket costs of between $18,759 and $36,279.

The operation of the airplane, it was assumed, would be approximately equal to travel by alternative modes. As the examples have shown, an actual savings would likely result over alternate modes, or the use of the airplane would not have been chosen. Even though these savings will almost surely be real, they have been assumed away as a conservative bias in the financial analysis.

It is left to XYZ Company to weigh the relative value of 3,048 man-hours, 1,048 man-hours of employee time, 414 overnight stays, an apparent actual dollar cost saving of the aircraft over the airlines/automobile mode of transportation, and the many intangi-

VALUE-ANALYSIS WRAP-UP

TRIP	TRIPS/YEAR	AIRLINES/ AUTOMOBILE		CESSNA 340 ii		SAVINGS	
		TRIP	YEAR	TRIP	YEAR	TRIP	YEAR
Man-hours:							
A	126	20:00	2,520	6:20	798	13:40	1,772
B	45	18:36	792	11:32	519	6:04	273
C	54	41:00	2,214	20:30	1107	19:30	1,107
Totals	225		5,526		2424		3,102 Man-hrs saved
Man RONs							
A	126	2	252	0	0	2	252
B	45	0	0	0	0	0	0
C	54	3	162	0	0/0	3	162
Totals	225		414				414 Man RONs saved
Morale time							
A	126	8:00	1,008	:00	0	8:00	1,008
B	45	9:06	409	1:36	72	7:30	337
C	54	:00	0	5:30	297	(5:30)	(297)
Totals	225		1,417		297		1,048 Moral hours saves

Table 18-20. Value Analysis Wrap-Up.

ble benefits associated with private aircraft against the additional $18,759 to $36,279 average cost increase associated with ownership. These 3,048 man-hours, compared to 5,472 man-hours involved in XYZ Company's present travel, represent a potential 56-percent increase in travel productivity.

Intangible Benefits

Of what is time made? In the world of business and commerce it is made of money, wages by the hour, salaries by the week, profits by the quarter and taxes by the year. The businessman sitting in an airline terminal, waiting for a delayed flight, is throwing away time and money.

Time and money are discovered and used by the businessman in his own aircraft en route to an appointment. No matter what the particular mission of a business aircraft is, the ultimate reasons for its use are the same. Save time otherwise lost in the dead space of traveling by inflexibility scheduled means. Make time otherwise lost due to the "you can't get there from here" syndrome of airline route systems. Compress time so that an hour-long transaction out of town does not require an overnight stay. Expand time so that productivity is greater.

It is generally known that top decision makers in a corporation are in a position to weigh the relative importance of intangible benefits such as convenience, comfort or even prestige. The reason for this is that the decision makers are generally also the users of the aircraft. They recognize that the intangible rather than the tangible factors usually provide the margin of profit in business aircraft use. Accountants and comptrollers may wish to be shown actual cost savings in dollars as well as increased productivity that can be measured. Their evaluations will eventually become major determinants in all major business aircraft purchase decisions. There still remain, however, the areas of subjectivity and judgement, especially in regard to the worth of an executive's time to his company and the value placed on intangible benefits.

No universal means has been devised, as yet, to measure the benefits of these intangibles which are so readily and universally accepted and existing. These intangibles are, however, becoming major determining factors in aircraft decisions, and rightfully so. Orthodox cost-savings analyses should not outweigh astute business judgment which considers all factors, including those which don't show up on the usual cost-savings analysis.

Table 18-21. A Do-It-Yourself Capital-Recovery Guide to Aid in Determining the Financial Effects of Aircraft Ownership on a Business or Corporation.

NOTE: The form below may help you estimate your net capital investment, based on depreciation factors for business use and the personal tax saving involved. This abbreviated form is not intended as tax advice, and it is recommended that you check your figures with your accountant or tax advisor... or have him work the figures for you.

INSTRUCTIONS:

Just fill in the column at the right of the page. For an explanation of methods used, or meaning of terms, see EXPLANATORY NOTES on reverse side.

LINE NO.	SUBJECT	HOW TO FIGURE	
Line 1:	Cost of new airplane*		$ _____
Line 2:	DEPRECIATION over 6 years. Choose your own depreciation method. Multiply Line 1 figure x % of depreciation you expect to take on this equipment in the next 6 years. Enter this dollar figure on Line 2.*		$ _____
Line 3:	Trade-in Value After 6 Years. This factor requires that you look into the future to see what your aircraft will be worth. Your Beechcraft Salesman can help you determine a reasonable trade-in value, based on his knowledge of your aircraft. Historical data from such sources as published official price guides of the Aircraft Dealers Service Assn. may also be of assistance. These have shown that BEECHCRAFT Products consistently retain more value.		$ _____
	7-YEAR CASH RECOVERY from/TAX SAVINGS, etc.		
Line 4:	Investment Tax Credit for 6 years (Line 1 x 6.667%)*		$ _____
Line 5:	Tax Savings on Depreciation (Line 2 x your top tax %)*		_____

214

Line 6	Trade-in Value after 6 years (Figure from Line 3)*	
Line 7	TOTAL COST RECOVERED (Add Lines 4 + 5 + 6)	$
Line 8	Original Cost of Airplane (Line 1 figure)	$
Line 9	Cost Recovered (Line 7 figure)	$
Line 10	NET COST. 6 years (Subtract Line 9 from Line 8)	$
Line 11	NET COST per YEAR (Line 10 ÷ 6)	$
Line 12	NET COST per MONTH (Line 11 ÷ 12)	$

EXPLANATORY NOTES

Line 1: Cost of figuring trade-in values are not included in this quick-figuring Guide, because of wide range of variables — amount of cash down payment, length of financing periods, rate of interest, etc.

Line 2: Depreciation for tax purposes has been based on the plane being used 100% for business. If used partly for personal, then multiply the percentage of business use times the amount on Line 2 for allowable tax depreciation. A 5- to 7-year life is suggested by the Internal Revenue Service, under the liberalized depreciation policy. For the basis of this analysis a 6-year life is used. (Use of one of the accelerated methods of depreciation would provide an earlier recovery of capital. Also, your experience may indicate a different depreciable life.)

Line 4: Under the current tax bill, property with a useful life of 3-4 years qualifies for 3.333% investment tax credit. Property with a useful life of 5-6 years qualifies for 6.667% investment tax credit and property with a useful life of 7 years or more qualifies for the full 10% investment tax credit.

Line 5: Tax Savings on Depreciation.* For quick estimating purposes you can use the following 1977 scale on personal income tax brackets for a married couple filing a joint return. State and city income tax percentages, along with surtax (if any) should be added to the federal percentages shown.

$ 11,900-$ 16,000	1,404 plus 21% on all over	$ 11,900
16,000- 20,200	2,265 plus 24% on all over	$ 16,000
20,200- 24,600	3,273 plus 28% on all over	$ 20,200
24,600- 29,900	4,505 plus 32% on all over	$ 24,600
29,900- 35,200	6,201 plus 37% on all over	$ 29,900
35,200- 45,800	8,162 plus 43% on all over	$ 35,200
45,800- 60,000	12,720 plus 49% on all over	$ 45,800
60,000- 85,600	19,678 plus 54% on all over	$ 60,000
85,600- 109,400	33,502 plus 59% on all over	$ 85,600
109,400- 162,400	47,544 plus 64% on all over	$109,400
162,400- 215,400	81,464 plus 68% on all over	$162,400
Over 215,400	117,504 plus 70% on all over	$215,400
FOR CORPORATIONS	49% on all over	$100,000

Line 6: Trade-in Value after 6 years. If plane is sold outright (instead of traded) then the excess of the selling price over book value is subject to tax. If the selling price is less than book value, a capital loss is reflected.

The business aircraft's efficiency depends on the wisdom with which it is employed. The aircraft can range from a valuable cost-savings and profit making tool to a pure cost center incapable of revenue or profits, depending upon its utilization. With modern business methods this under-utilization rarely occurs. Utilization of an aircraft is the basis for productivity. Here is where time values become so important. Each firm should establish its own basis for calculation of the man-hour/worth coefficient.

Obviously, where cost is a trade off against time, several factors must be weighed. Among them are the intrinsic value of the person or cargo to be moved, the emergency need for travel to be accomplished, the perishable nature or deterioration rate of a situation, and any seasonable or peak-demand requirement.

In the same light, convenience is a major intangible closely related to time savings. Convenience means more than niceties. It means flexibility. Convenience results in simplification of travel from point to point. It provides morale benefits.

Comfort is another major item. Its meaningfulness stems from the relationship of comfort to fatigue and the attendant effect fatigue has on productivity.

Other Factors

There are naturally many other intangibles to business aircraft use. These include but are not limited to the following:

—The ability to minimize additional personnel requirements by increasing the executive's area of control.

—Increased sales through more frequent face-to-face contact with customers.

—The flexibility of scheduling and destinations, thereby providing increased ability to stay even with or ahead of competition.

—Increased flexibility and ability to get to the out-of-the-way places.

—The ability to make extra hours available for business and other activities by reducing unproductive travel time to a minimum.

—Avoidance of ticketing and security queues, missed connections, late flights, luggage lines, and highway delays in getting to the airport.

—Additional compensation for employees in a highly competitive work force.

—Improved customer relations and service through increased communication.

—Increased ability to attract and employ key personnel in competition with others in your field.

—Pure travel convenience.

—Providing of shorter reaction time to new business opportunities.

—Conveyance of the image of an efficient, well-run company, thereby gaining prestige and securing client confidence.

—A more efficient way to handle the emergency need to travel.

—The ability to meet emergency situations regarding transportation of personnel and/or cargo.

—The morale factor of not being constantly on the road.

—The ability to have business discussions in your own private en-route conference room.

—Lowering the chance of travel fatigue and the attendant effects fatigue has on productivity.

—Pure business entertainment.

—Increased productivity resulting from greater travel mobility.

—Fewer nights away from home and family.

—Availability of a superior travel service (for discretionary use) for customers whose time is valuable.

The utilization of a business aircraft is marked by flexibility. Its acquisition allows the company the freedom to tailor the aircraft to its needs. As the complexity of modern business continues to change and the demands for more efficiency increase, the requirements for judgmental decisions increase.

Continuing curtailment of flight schedules by scheduled airlines and the growing inability or unwillingness of regional carriers to service low density points compound the problems attendant to company travel needs. That leaves business air transportation as premium transportation (Table 18-21).

Glossary Of Terms

Accelerate-stop distance: The distance required, under standard atmospheric conditions and with no wind, to accelerate an aircraft to liftoff speed and then to come to a full stop, using heavy breaking.

ADF: Automatic direction finder.

ADF approach: A non-precision instrument approach which uses a non-directional beacon or a standard broadcast station for primary navigational guidance.

aerostar: A family of piston twins developed by the late Ted Smith, and now manufactured and marketed by Piper Aircraft Corporation.

agl: Above ground level.

Agusta 109A: A twin-turbine helicopter manufactured by Giovanni Agusta in Italy.

Alouette: A family of single-turbine helicopters manufactured by Aerospatiale in France.

AOPA: Aircraft Owners and Pilots Association.

Aries T-250: A T-tailed high-performance single-engine aircraft manufactured by Bellanca Aircraft Corporation.

AStar: A single-turbine helicopter manufactured by Aerospatiale in France.

ATC: Air-traffic control.

Baron: A family of piston twins manufactured by Beech Aircraft Corporation.

Bonanza: A popular high performance single-engine aircraft manufactured by Beech Aircraft Corporation.

cabin-class twins: Piston-engine aircraft in which the cockpit is usually separated from the passenger compartments; an aisle between seats permits getting up and moving around in flight.

CAT II: Category II landing minimums, lower than normal (Category I) IFR landing minimums.

Cessna Citation: A family of corporate jet aircraft manufactured by Cessna Aircraft Company.

Cessna 172: Cessna Skyhawk.

Cessna Pressurized Centurion: The only single-engine pressurized aircraft on the market today. Manufactured by Cessna Aircraft Company.

Cessna Skywagon: A family of six and seven-seat high performance fixed-gear single-engine aircraft manufactured by Cessna Aircraft Company.

Cessna 310: A piston twin, manufactured by Cessna Aircraft Company.

Challenger: A corporate jet with intercontinental range, manufactured by Canadair, Ltd., in Canada.

Chancellor: A pressurized piston twin manufactured by Cessna Aircraft Company.

Cheyenne: A family of turboprop aircraft manufactured by Piper Aircraft Corporation.

Chinook: A twin-rotor helicopter manufactured by Boeing Vertol.

Conquest: A turboprop manufactured by Cessna Aircraft Company.

Consumables: Fuel and oil.

Conventional gear: Tail-wheel aircraft in which the center of gravity is to the rear of the main gear.

Dakota: A fixed-gear high performance single-engine aircraft manufactured by Piper Aircraft Corporation.

Dauphin: A family of turbine helicopters manufactured by Aerospatiale in France.

DME: Distance-measuring equipment.

EJA: Executive Jet Aviation.

ETA: Estimated time of arrival.

Executive: A family of turboprop aircraft manufactured by Rockwell International.

Falcon 10, 20, 50: A family of corporate jet aircraft manufactured by Marcel Dassault-Breguet in France.

fanjets: A jet engine which, in addition to producing jet thrust, drives a shrouded fan. It is quieter and more fuel efficient than a turbojet engine.

FARs: Federal Aviation Regulations.

FBO: Fixed-base operator.

fpm: Feet per minute.

FSS: Flight-service station.

GI, GII, GIII: Aircraft manufactured originally by Grumman Aviation. The GI was a turboprop and is no longer in production. The GII and GIII are corporate jets with intercontinental range. They are now being manufactured by Gulfstream American Corporation.

gph: Gallons per hour.

Gulfstream I, II, III: See GI, GII, GIII.

HIGE: Hovering in ground effect (ceiling).

High bypass engine: A fanjet engine.

high-performance single: A term generally applied to single-engine aircraft with a variable-pitch propeller.

Hobbs meter: A cockpit instrument which records the time during which the main switch of the aircraft was in the ON position.

HOGE: Hovering out of ground effect (ceiling).

ICAO: International Civil Aviation Organization.

IFR: Instrument flight rules.

IRS: Internal Revenue Service.

ITC: Investment tax credit.

Jeppesen: Manufacturer of aviation charts. The term is also used for the charts themselves.

King Air: A family of turboprop aircraft manufactured by Beech Aircraft Corporation.

knot: Nautical miles per hour.

Lama: A tubine helicopter manufactured by Aerospatiale in France.

Lance: A high-performance single-engine six-seat aircraft with retractable gear and T-tail, manufactured by Piper Aircraft Corporation.

lbs: Pounds.

Learjet: A family of corporate jets, manufactued by Gates Learjet Corporation.

Long Ranger: A single-turbine helicopter, manufactured by Bell Helicopters.

M/E: Multi-engine.

MEA: Minimum en-rout altitude.

Mooney 201: A high performance single-engine four-seat aircraft with retractable gear. Manufactured by Mooney Aircraft Corporation.

Mooney 231: The turbo charged version of the Mooney 201.

mpg: Miles per gallon.

msl: Height above mean sea level.

Navajo: A family of cabin-class piston twins manufactured by Piper Aircraft Corporation.

NBAA: National Business Aircraft Association.

NDB: Non-directional beacon.

nm: Nautical mile.

normally aspirated: A non-turbocharged piston engine.

OBI: Omni-bearing indicator.

owner-flown twins: Generally four or six-seat piston-engine twins with no room in the cabin to walk around in flight.

Piper Cheyenne: A family of turboprop aircraft manufactured by Piper Aircraft Corporation.

pph: Pounds per hour.

pressurization: A means of keeping the atmospheric pressure inside the cabin higher than it is outside the cabin.

psi: Pounds per square inch.

pure jet: Turbo jet or fan jet, as opposed to turboprop or propjet.

Ranger: A high performance single-engine aircraft with retractable gear and four seats, manufactured by Mooney Aircraft Corporation.

RNAV: Area navigation.

ROC: Rate of climb.

Rockwell Alpine Commander: A turbocharged single-engine aircraft, no longer in production.

Rockwell Shrike Commander: A piston twin, usually thought of as in the owner-flown category, despite the fact that in its cabin the cockpit and the passenger compartment are separate. Manufactured by Rockwell International.

ROI: Return on investment.

RON: Rest (or remain) overnight.

rpm: Revolutions per minute.

SAS: Stability augmentation system. A type of autopilot designed specifically for helicopters.

S/E: Single engine.

Sensca II: A turbocharged six-seat piston twin manufactured by Piper Aircraft Corporation.

service ceiling: The altitude at which an aircraft, at gross, under standard atmospheric condition, is still able to climb at 100 fpm.

shrouded propeller: A propeller or fan with a covering around the outside.

Skyhawk: A fixed-gear single-engine aircraft, the most popular single aircraft type ever, manufactured by Cessna Aircraft Company.

Solitaire: A turboprop aircraft, the fastest of all, manufactured by Mitsubishi Aircraft International.

Spirit: The twin-turbine S-76 helicopter manufactured by Sikorsky Aircraft Division.

taildragger: Aircraft equipped with a conventional gear.

TAS: True airspeed.

TBO: Time between major engine overhauls.

TC: Turbocharged.

TCA: Terminal control area.

tricycle gear: A gear with the third wheel under the nose of the aircraft and with the aircraft's center of gravity ahead of the main gear.

turbocharged: A means of feeding compressed air to a piston engine, permitting it to develop sea-level power up to high altitudes.

turbojets: The basic jet engine, using pure thrust for propulsion. Turbojets have no fans.

turboprop: An aircraft equipped with jet engines which drive a shaft to which a propeller is attached. The engines are also known as turboshaft engines.

212: A twin-turbine helicopter, manufactured by Bell Helicopters.

222: A twin-turbine executive transport helicopter manufactured by Bell Helicopters.

usable fuel: The amount of fuel in the tanks which will be fed to the engine regardless of the attitude of the aircraft. All aircraft have a certain amount of so-called unusable fuel which would feed to the engine only if the aircraft maintains at a straight-and-level attitude.

VFR: Visual flight rules.

Victor Airway: Airways defined by VORs, at altitudes from the ground up to but not including 18,000 feet.

VOR: Very high frequency omni-directional radio range.

VTOL: Vertical takeoff and landing (aircraft).

wet rate: The rental rate for aircraft which includes fuel and oil.

Index